Wait a Minute,
I Have to Take Off My Bra

Betty Dobson, Editor
Darcelle Adams-Frank, Associate Editor

InkSpotter Publishing

Wait a Minute,

I Have to Take Off My Bra

PUBLISHED BY INKSPOTTER PUBLISHING
163 Main Avenue, Halifax, Nova Scotia, Canada B3M 1B3
http://inkspotter.com/

Cover photograph © 2011 Robert R. Sanders
RobertSandersPhoto.com

Printed and bound in the United States of America by CreateSpace

ISBN 978-0-9813335-1-9

Also available from InkSpotter Publishing:

The August Gale (2010)
Baby Angels (2010)
Backless, Strapless & Slit to the Throat (2009)
A Boy Named Wish (2009)
Collywobblers (2008)
The Communal Desk (2009)
Dangerous Curves (2011)
Family Lines (2009)
Holiday Writes (2007)
Paper Wings (2006)

Contents

Foreword

Betty Dobson

Can you judge a book by its cover? Sometimes.

Can you judge *this* book by its cover? I think you can.

One of the main reasons for publishing this anthology is to celebrate something that is so distinctly female yet often treated with disrespect. Robert Sanders stunning photograph conveys that message with both style and substance. (A special thank you goes out to poet Shawn Aveningo for bringing the image to us in the first place.)

This book grew out of a conversation with one of my best friends, Darcelle Adams-Frank. After toying with few project ideas without ever finding one that fit, we finally sat down to brainstorm a complete and workable plan. We knew we wanted to publish an anthology and that we wanted to donate part of the proceeds to charity. We also decided we wanted something of relevance to women. Breasts—and breast cancer research—easily fit the bill.

We considered dozens of potential titles before settling on *Wait a Minute, I Have to Take Off My Bra*. As working women, we both knew the distinct pleasure of getting our bras off the moment we walked through the front door after a long day at the office.

In terms of promoting a charity, breast cancer research instantly resonated with me. I grew up with a keen awareness of breast cancer. My mother was diagnosed with the first of six benign tumours when she was thirty-five. I also appreciated how lucky she was.

In grade seven, I discovered a lump in my own breast. When I told my mother, she looked as if I'd just sucked the life out of her. Her face fell. And she whispered,

"You're too young." In another stroke of luck, my lump turned out to be a cyst. No biopsy. No surgery. No fear of malignancy. Plus, I learned exactly what to look for in future self breast examinations. I knew what a lump really felt like.

I think it goes without saying that breast cancer has touched everyone's life in one way or another. Based on that universality and judging by the early response to this anthology—to the mere fact of its impending publication—I have high hopes that we'll reach a wide readership and raise lots of money for a worthy cause.

The Breast Cancer Society of Canada is our charity of choice, and we thank you for helping us support their efforts.

How to Buy a Bra When You Have Changed Weight
Jenni L. Ivins

My friend, who recently lost weight, just emailed to tell me that she bought—and was now strutting around in—a new bra. She wrote: "Sorry if I sound excited, but I am. Sad but true." She was wondering how others who were losing poundage handled the female question of parts not staying where they were put.

I, too, was familiar with the problem and was relieved to hear that I wasn't abnormal in this. I stopped mentioning the issue to my thinner friends, however, as they just looked at me pitifully and shook their heads. Not comforting at all when I needed reassurance.

I don't know why breasts can't just lie comfortably in their cups rather than bungee like a pair of tennis balls in tights when one moves. Not that they look like that when I stand naked in front of the mirror. Of course, I do stand with my shoulders well back at such times, and, since I'm usually about to step into the shower, I don't have my glasses on, so my perspective might be affected by imagination and mood.

Unfortunately, the only way I found to resolve the peek-a-boo problem to which my friend referred was the same way that she did—by buying a *newwww* bra! {Said *Price is Right* style, please.}

However, this creates a new dilemma: how to explain the bumps in the dressing room when I am choosing said item of underwear. Pre weight changes, the ritual was to adjust the straps to my estimated size then lean forward, ensuring that the bra cupped my breasts before fastening the hooks and eyes. Now I also lift my arms a few times

1

and move them from side to side. I jump up and down, my hands held high above my head. Then I throw in a few diaphragm expanding exercises that you may or may not recognise as the actions that go with "I must, I must, I must increase my bust."

All of this exertion often leads to a bit of curtain bumping, huffing and puffing—and heightened facial colour when I leave the fitting room. But I leave feeling confident that my breasts will stay in their place and not venture out unexpectedly.

I relayed my experience to my friend, comforted by the knowledge that she would understand.

We should enjoy our new bras, stand proud, and feel secure as we strut with aplomb.

Pink Ribbons

Shawn Aveningo

One lump or two?
Ma'am....your coffee?
One lump or two?
Such an innocent question
uttered hundreds of times
in tea rooms, coffee houses,
restaurants, airplanes.

Today, those words
had the power
to bring her to her knees.
No amount of chamomile
or honey capable
of soothing her pain.
She was drowning
in a sea of sorrow,
fearful of what
tomorrow would bring.

How could she face
this new reflection,
scarred, disfigured?
What would she see
reflecting in his eyes?
He said he would always
love her, no matter what.
He said she would always
be beautiful to him,
but this....this

3

isn't what crosses your
mind, vowing in
sickness and health.

Each day she'll carry on,
with a stiff upper lip
and pink ribbons in her hair,
stuffing the prosthetic
into her bra, no longer
adorned with sheer lace.
She'll march with an
army of women.

She's grateful to be
among the living,
a survivor as she's
now known. But she misses
her curves, even if sometimes
they sagged. She misses
the tingling of her nipples
when her husband held
her in his arms. She
misses feeling like a woman.
She misses feeling
whole.

Ma'am?
One lump or two?
She replied,
Oh, No Thank You.
No lumps for me.

34B

Mary MacGowan

I told my children the night before—
they paraded around the kitchen
with pointy paper cups
on their chests.

Now, beach towels
strategically placed over railings,
I slouch low in an Adirondack chair,
untie my top and let them go free.

My breasts and I follow the one
shot of sun that comes in through
tall white pines; my chair scrapes
as we skootch across the deck.

Sun and leaf-shadow
warm and cool them,
plumped and fondled
by every passing breeze.

No sense denying it:
someday I'll be gone,
and two plastic bags
will sit atop dry rib bones.

Here I am, now, wondering
if thieves are stealing
a glimpse, and if I care,
and if I ever cared.

Silvery Fish

Sharon Burton

Sitting on my porch in the sunshine on a warm, soft afternoon, I read the letter in my hand again. It continues to say—and I've read it many times in the last ninety seconds—that the results of my mammogram are not normal. Specifically, my left breast is not playing nicely and needs to go back for additional testing. Such as an ultrasound, the letter says.

Ultrasound, I think. My left breast.

I read the letter again, in case I'm missing some important words, like "This Letter is a Mistake." I read every word again, several times, and they're all the same words in all the same order. Thoughts occur to me, the first of which is that running in circles and pulling out my hair like mad woman is a good idea. What I actually do, though, is cup my left breast in my hand and hold it against me, gently, the way I would a hurt child.

This is not good. That's the next thought.

My mother died from breast cancer. I started annual mammograms several years ago, when I was thirty-six or thirty-eight years old, to catch bad things early. Until this moment, mammograms were my talisman against just this sort of result. My agreement with the universe was that I did what my mother didn't do, thereby preventing the bad thing from happening to me. Cancer cells invaded my mother's body like tiny silver fishes, darting from breasts to liver to bones, darting too fast to catch.

I might have fishes. In my left breast.

I want my breasts just as they were, in a generally

7

matched, soft, squishy pair on my chest.

I can do without one or both, if I have to, I think. If it's a choice between them or me, they can go. But losing one or both is suddenly a terrible idea. I want breasts, my breasts, just like last year, without fishes.

I'm afraid of my breasts.

I stand up, wobbling like a sailor trying to get her land legs, and go inside. I need to call the clinic and make an appointment. The letter includes a number to call, but it's a menu number. Radiology or Silvery Fishes in Breasts are not options, even though I press seven to hear the menu again. Frustrated, I hang up. I'm gasping. I breathe, in and out. Calm, calm, I think. This is not an emergency. Yet. This is a phone call for an appointment. I can do this. Call back and press zero to get the operator. She can send me to Radiology.

This is how it starts.

With my mother, it was like this.

I make the appointment. A week from now. Only a week worries me.

I waited six weeks for the original appointment.

Now, suddenly, there are no breasts left to examine, and all the appointments are open? I think I'm on a special list now—or at least my left breast is.

I don't want to be afraid for me.

In the bathroom, I take off my shirt and my bra. I look at myself in the mirror. I compare breasts: left, right, and left again. They look no different than this morning, pre-letter, post-shower. I poke and prod, looking for fishes or lumps...either one...both...but I feel nothing different. Nothing swimming or darting. They still hang gently, like soft water balloons.

My left breast, I think. Ultrasound.

This could be anything: a cyst, a nothing, a fish, a something. It's the uncertainty, the wait until next week. I pull my bra and my shirt back on, gently placing my left breast in the lace cup.

Faded Rose Tattoo[1]
Betty Dobson

she's like her faded rose tattoo
youth's sigil on her breast
paled from the centre
colour worn away
with the flesh
petals fallen
or plucked
in fits of love
<love me not>
her withered stem
bowed before time
and distended leaves
courted only by gravity
tempted by the blade
pruning and grafting
(winter's harbinger)
like wiring the bud
for two more days'
worth of show, illusion
cast in a rose-cut image

[1] Previously published in *Epiphanies and Other Absurdities* (The Writers' Association, 2005)

Examining My Breasts

Barbara Daniels

Some women wait till their tumors bulge
like oranges. They juggle their breasts
into their dresses, never look, never touch,
wait months till they see a doctor
in Oklahoma City, go home in the pickup
the day of the surgery, make Thanksgiving dinner
with draining tubes tucked in their clothes.

I knew a woman who threw away garter belts
and push-up bras so her children wouldn't
have to after she died. She called a doctor
the day she found the lump, walked out
on the grass to talk with her surgeon,
did what he told her, and died
though she was careful. Anyone can.

When I lift my arms, veins in my armpits
twine in a web. I slide my fingers
over my breasts. I fear cul de sacs,
no way out. I make myself follow
the shuddering paths, brush my way in
where a spider might wait,
one foot testing a sticky strand.

My Refined Bosom

Mary Zelinka

One day back in the Fifties, when I was in second grade, I stuffed two oranges up my shirt. Keeping my pretend breasts in place by holding my shirttail tight, I danced around the house, giggling. Even my mother laughed.

As I grew older, Mother confided her hopes that I would be small-breasted like her side of the family rather than inherit the large breasts of my father's Ukrainian mother. "A large bosom is not refined," she explained.

But I was too busy hunting the lizards that hid in the hibiscus hedge around our Miami house to give breasts much thought.

Then, the summer before seventh grade, I became aware of that tantalizing stripe crossing the backs of the older girls...the bewitching sign of a brassiere. I wanted a stripe across my back, too—that mysterious line meant being a grownup.

I didn't get my brassiere until months later, after I turned twelve.

Even then Mother was reluctant. "You have nothing to put into a brassiere! What about a sweet little undershirt with flowers?"

"No!" I sobbed. "Everybody in seventh grade has one! I want one, too!"

At last she gave in, and I proudly walked off to school wearing my first brassiere. The squashed cups where my breasts would go someday made the front of my shirt lumpy, but that was a small price to pay for the coveted stripe across my back. I tried not to breathe too deeply to

13

keep the elastic from creeping up my chest and spoiling the effect.

I paraded down the hall to my homeroom, twisting my back by a group of girls so they would notice my grown-up stripe. Then I slid into my seat and leaned back, waiting for the secrets of adulthood to wash over me.

Snap!

"*Ow!*" I spun around and glared into Wayne's grinning face.

"Mary's-got-a-bra-siere-Mary's-got-a-bra-siere,"   he sing-songed.

"Cut it out!" I hissed, narrowing my eyes at him. I turned back around, sucking in my breath and swiggling my chest, trying to manoeuvre the brassiere back where it was supposed to be. Finally, I grabbed the bottom of it with my fingers and tugged it down.

Wayne snickered.

By the end of the day, exhausted from the combination of shallow breathing and running to the girls' room to adjust my brassiere, the magical stripe across my back had lost its charm. The minute I got home, I wadded it up and stuffed it in the back of my underwear drawer, praying for my bosom to stay refined.

But by the end of the school year, my hunched shoulders could no longer hide the persistent new buds on my chest. Mother insisted I wear my brassiere, and, for the next five years, until I graduated from high school, my tiny breasts were bound by cotton cups and elastic, which was forever creeping into my armpits.

In the cold climate of Colorado, where I went to college, no one could tell I wasn't wearing a brassiere under my shirt and heavy sweater. The freedom of being braless made up for being the flat-chested one among my three roommates—each of whom could have easily passed for having oranges under her shirt.

After a while, I didn't care whether anyone knew I was wearing a brassiere or not and threw them all out. By the time going braless was fashionable, I hadn't worn one for years.

Then one day when I was in my mid-thirties, a lacy, flesh-coloured brassiere on display in a boutique caught my attention. The cups were cut daringly low, and it fastened with a cunning little hook between the breasts. I fell in love with it immediately and wore it the next day, feeling sexy and mysterious.

But at the grocery store after work, the hook popped open in the checkout line, snapping the cups into my armpits. Hunching into *The National Enquirer*, I tried repositioning the brassiere and fastening it without anyone noticing, but the elastic kept whipping the cups apart.

Finally giving up, I reached up my left sleeve, pulled the strap down over my crooked elbow, dragged the brassier out through the other sleeve, and stuffed it into my purse. Ignoring the astonished looks of the checker, the bag boy, and the customers in line behind me, I paid for my groceries and swept out of the store.

Now in my sixties, I am still braless—although my breasts are no longer perky. I remain grateful that my bosom, at least, is refined.

Mammogram

Barbara Daniels

I have the vertical scar, the jaggy
sideways scar and the new little
half-moon scar, the one on my breast.

I didn't know I could murder vermin,
shovel their bodies into the trash.
That's where my tumors went

and the septic gall bladder and ball
of breast fat—not cancer, not this
time. At South Jersey Radiology,

I pull one arm from a wrinkled salmon
hospital gown, then the other, squeeze
my more-or-less healthy breasts into

images, stand quietly, holding my breath.
My technician is doing sacred work,
checking numbers, touching her hair.

She asks me about the weather. Her room
is windowless but I bring news of wind,
sun, the finch as a leading indicator

of a new season, spring, finally, truly
spring. I go home to mice in the walls.
I am Death for them. I can kill.

Pillow

Patricia Wellingham-Jones

Your mouth twists,
tears spill hot down your face.
I reach out,
draw you to my breast.
Run my hands
down your long silky hair.
Your young head
rests against hard bone
instead of soft pillows.
I sigh, as I haven't for years,
at the small comfort
the knife removed
while saving my life.

Seeing Pink
J.M. Cornwell

The only things that got my mother's attention were the length of my skirts (hems must be below the knees) and necklines (nothing must show below the collar bone). She constantly prodded me to "sit up straight" or "stand up straight" until I responded without thinking. Chin up, chest out, back straight, jaw tensed, teeth grinding, and smile tense.

One Saturday morning while I lay in bed, Mom burst into my bedroom. "Get up out of that bed and go wash under your arms. They're filthy."

"I took a bath last night."

She grabbed my arm. "How lazy can you...?" She stared at my armpit. "Get dressed," she said as she left. She finally noticed the hair growing in my armpits.

Less than a month later, while standing in line outside my sixth grade classroom waiting for the teacher, the fact I was growing up shook me.

I wore my mother's favourite, a two-piece sailor outfit: navy blue pleated skirt and thin white sweater with a red scarf knotted at the neck. Rob Stokes acted up, making us laugh until...

"I can see your nipples," he crowed, "and they're pink."

The boys crowded closer. The girls moved away.

"Wow," Rob said, "they're really pink. See?" He pointed at my chest.

I crossed my arms over my chest and glared. "Your barn door is open." Rob checked his zipper. I gritted my teeth and swallowed hard to keep the tears back, hunching shoulders to hide my chest.

When my mother got home from work, I told her I needed new clothes.

"We just bought you new clothes for school."

"My clothes are too tight."

"You look fine," she said in her "that's final" voice.

"I have to have new clothes," I said before the story tumbled out in a rush.

My mother looked at me as though seeing me for the first time. Her hand flew to her mouth, and she stepped back. "Stand up straight." I snapped to attention: chest out, chin up, shoulders back. "Oh," she said with a look of shock in her eyes. "Go peel the potatoes for dinner."

The subject was closed.

I dug out all my old tee shirts, locked the bathroom door, and tried them on. They made my chest ache. Nothing fit. I took an old undershirt from Dad's dresser drawer, balled it up, and snuck upstairs. After I closed and locked the bathroom door, off came my top, and the undershirt went on and down and down until it cascaded past my knees. Mom's bras were impossibly huge, and the foam rubber breasts in the bottom of the buffet made me look top heavy and lopsided. I wanted camouflage, not bigger breasts.

"Please, God, make Mom buy me bigger clothes," I prayed each night. I put my legs through the arms of my sweaters in hopes of stretching them, but the seams ripped. Mom complained about the mending.

"I must be growing really fast," I said hopefully.

"Wear something else," my mother ordered.

Clothing choices shrank, the mending pile grew, and Dad's undershirt looked better and better.

"Where's the top that goes to this?" Mom held up the navy blue pleated skirt.

"I don't know."

She tossed an armload of clothes onto the bed. "Hang those up. We'll clean out that closet later."

The white knit top had to go, maybe into the trash barrel under the ashes and rusted tin cans. Meanwhile, holey sheets destined for dusting rags, held on with safety pins, wrapped my chest, but either the pins stuck me or the binding slipped slowly down to my hips. The hard little knots on my chest got bigger, and I slouched to hide them.

Christmas vacation came and brought a whole week of wearing play clothes, and no one to worry about my chest...until Christmas morning.

We crept down the stairs in the dark toward the black triangle of the tree whispering in the foyer and getting as close as we dared.

Mom appeared in the living room, her face shiny in the nightlight. "Get back upstairs."

We went as far as the top landing, hunkered down and waited.

"I said, get back upstairs."

We went. Huddled together on my bed, we whispered and waited and anxiously watched for the first faint flags of dawn.

As we finally gathered around the lighted tree, patiently waiting for our gifts, Mom and Dad handed out presents until the only box left was the one Mom held on her lap.

Dad hovered.

Mom smiled.

I hesitated. Probably clothes. I opened the box and resisted the urge to toss it and run.

On top of a navy blue sweater was a bra, a real bra with hooks and straps—and cups. The cups were rumpled cotton mounds of air and cloth with rigid circles of stitching pointing up at me.

Mom and Dad beamed.

I cringed inside.

"Go put it on," Mom urged.

"But I wanted to..."

"We want to see if it fits," she said in her "obey or else" tone.

Like walking the last mile to the electric chair, I went to my room, put on the bra with my eyes closed, and looked down to where the full cups stuck out. I pulled the soft navy blue sweater over my head and smoothed it down over my pyjama bottoms. I stared down at the front of the sweater where it swelled softly over the bra, over me in the bra. I couldn't go to school like this. There would be talk of Kleenex stuffing and foam rubber boobs.

"Don't take all day," my mother yelled.

Down in the living room, my sisters giggled, and I slouched past and went into my parents' room.

"Let's have a look. Stand up straight," Mom ordered.

I snapped to attention: head up, chin out, shoulders back. Flames engulfed my cheeks and the tips of my ears.

"Turn around."

I moved slowly.

"She won't wear that long." Mom pulled up the back of my sweater and checked the hooks. She spun me around.

"You look all grown up," Dad said. For the first time, I smiled a real smile and stood up straight without urging.

Back in school, Rob Stokes asked, "Were you always this tall?"

I smiled and sat down at my desk.

Child of the West

Patricia Wellingham-Jones

Sue's new chariot
sports every fancy gadget,
leans back at many angles,
almost serves drinks.
She rides it into our writing group
at the cancer centre.

Instead of exclaiming
over her fancy new chair,
all we see are scabs and bruises
on her freckled face, her arms.

Seems the chariot rebelled
while trundling up the ramp to the van.
Flung itself and rider
onto the graveled road.

After that story is told
and the hugs and pats fade away,
we settle down to write.

Sue's tale that night
is about the horse she rode
when she was a Child of the West—
no MS, no wheelchair, no cancer
in her left breast—

and how she glowed with triumph
the day her skinny kid arms

could finally lift the big heavy saddle
way over her head
and onto the big horse.

Growth

Emily Hayes

He told her not to worry, he wasn't a boob man,
any more than a mouthful was way too much,
so she let him slip off her shirt and kiss
her nipples before he moved inside her
on the living room floor. Afterwards,
he cupped them in his hands and said
You make me want to be naked.

Tonight, a decade later, she stands braless
in their bedroom, a couple of weeks
into her second trimester, breasts swollen
two cup sizes, still sticking out farther
than her belly. He rubs the pads
of his thumbs across darkening areolas,
he traces the blue map of milk veins
with his tongue. She leaks colostrum
on his lips, and he tells her she tastes
like cantaloupe and papaya and bananas.

> ...This is the time of year when the smell of Bradford
> Pears has given way to lilac and honeysuckle blossoms,
> when marriage and babies might trump small breasts
> and sex, on an evening when the Pleiades nurse
> the Bull to blaze him home again...

Life Inside My Bra

Lois Jean Bousquet

I turn off the steamy spray and give my wet hair a final squeeze. Water droplets create a gauzy curtain on the translucent glass. I turn and wait, my fingers on the chrome door handle. Then my husband gives an appreciative wolf whistle. I reward him with a little burlesque shimmy. My right breast is the lone dancer in the routine, ignored by the adopted twin on her left, an ever-prim saline implant. I step out, reach for a towel, and Dennis whistles again. This little whistle-shimmy-whistle thing is our morning ritual, a gift to me nearly every day for the past twelve years. Back when it was new, before it was ritual, it took the sting out of the harsh surprise of breast cancer.

When I was coming of age, I was ignorant of cancer but painfully aware of tight sweaters and big boobs. Marilyn Monroe, Kim Novak, and Annette Funicello were objects of envy to starry-eyed girls and objects of lust to squeaky-voiced, hormonal boys. As I entered my teens, my breasts—no matter how much I pushed, prodded, and padded—evolved into only budding mounds. Whispered among naïve, flat-chested schoolgirls was a wishful myth that young busts were enlarged by the miracle of male hands. I married (young, naïve, and still flat-chested) and admitted defeat. The myth was just that. Then I got pregnant, and my hopes were raised once again. Motherhood was miraculous; as my belly got bigger, so did my bosom! My scoop-necked maternity wear actually showed cleavage, my first. At last I had woman-size breasts.

The ecstasy was short-lived. My respectable "C" sized Grandifloras shrank, and I returned my rosebuds to their padded push-ups.

By the late Seventies, I was a divorced thirty-something and banished my nylon bras to the dark corners of the lingerie drawer. I was not a feminist bra-burner, but cotton camisoles were less inhibiting—and who could tell, anyway? The new myth was that no one cared about the size of breasts anymore. Well, I did. Looking into mirrors, I paid little attention to my shapely legs or abundant auburn hair. What my fragile self-image saw reflected was a lack of cleavage for even the skimpiest swimsuit.

Life with my boobs changed in 1981. I married a man who taught me to love and respect all my body parts. Dennis convinced me that my little rosebuds were good! They filled his big hands perfectly! They had lovely pink tips! They jiggled enticingly. I became proud of their perky firmness, impertinent nipples and, yes, even enjoyed their diminutive size. I bought seductive lingerie, and I saw my body in a new way. At thirty-four, I finally felt sexy.

About ten years later, we were invited to a costume party. Our friends called us "the lovebirds," so we decided to go as a famous entangled couple. Warren Beatty's *Dick Tracy* movie had come out that year, so Dennis and I went to the party as the ruggedly handsome Tracy and the buxom bombshell Breathless. What a breakthrough for me, to poke fun at my figure as I stuffed and padded a borrowed bra to a colossal size D. We created quite an Oscar Night vision, Hollywood contenders for the famous line, "What does a girl have to do to get arrested?"—to which Tracy (a.k.a. Dennis) responds, "Wearing a dress like that is a step in the right direction." Then the dancing started, and we discovered that my new endowment kept us from our usual belt-polishing slow dancing! Returning home that night, first prize in hand, I gladly shed the top-heavy faux breasts to return to the real me.

In 1997, weeks after my fiftieth birthday, a mammogram showed breast cancer. Every morning I showered and towelled off and put on a fancy lace bra and worried. Would I survive—would we survive? Could I still be sexy when I became lopsided and mismatched?

Dennis was baffled by my worry. "Your breasts are beautiful—but they're what you look like, not who you are. It doesn't matter to me if you have two breasts, or one, or none at all. As long as I have you here with me."

I insulated myself in my husband's words and voraciously researched my options while the surgery calendar raced toward my date. My decision to have a breast implant was sheer vanity; I wanted to look balanced in my clothes. I added a second surgeon to my boob team, one who could pop in the replacement while I was still on the table. I read *The Breast Book* by Dr. Susan Love. I followed her advice and began paving my journey with humour and meditation. I called my mother and five sisters and told them to get their mammograms but not to worry because I had the statistics covered for all of us. My prescription for surgery was music—before, during, and after anaesthesia. To my surprise and relief, my two surgeons didn't think I was whacked out. They thought it was an awesome idea. I selected Pachelbel's *Canon* and began meditating daily.

I worked for a busy, high-tech firm, and my small department of five was close knit. Before my medical leave, we met to review the game plan for the eight weeks I'd be gone. The rather sombre mood was interrupted when Janet discreetly called my attention to a button undone on my blouse. I looked down at the small patch of flesh exposed above the white lace of my bra, aware of the silence.

"Oh well," I said. "Guess I better flaunt it while I got it!"

After a nanosecond of shock, the group burst into genuine laughter. The gloomy air brightened. Dr. Love would have been proud.

One day, just before my scheduled mastectomy, my meditation became a farewell to what was familiar. The house was quiet and summer smells floated in through the open windows. I put on my headset, lay down on the big floral sofa, and hugged a bed pillow while Pachelbel massaged my senses. I envisioned and welcomed my new body. Then, squeezing the pillow ever harder, I cried and cried, releasing the loss and grief and why-me and pity that washed up from toes to tear ducts.

This morning, standing in front of my full length mirror, I lift the soft warm flesh of my right breast to sit it higher in the bra cup. I adjust a half-moon of foam that's tucked under the left. My twins are no longer a matched set and these adjustments are an effort to achieve a semblance of symmetry. My implanted breast is shaped more like an egg yolk than the promised teardrop and sits too high I think. The other has lost that perky, headlight quality. But we're here together and we still draw whistles.

I pull my new pink sweater over my head and appraise the results. I nod. Good enough. Then I do another little shimmy—just because I can.

For a Small Girl Staring[2]

Christina Pacosz

How to tell you this is the tree
your body will grow into,
though you are a straight stick now
and I am dreaming
of falling down, decaying
slowly into duff.

Your body is reading my body
and you are open-mouthed,
clutching your Lilliputian suit,
while I towel my thighs dry.
My flesh, soft and spongy,
yours hard, early fruit.

My breasts, abundant at last,
are tipping toward you like bells
tolling, *the end, the end.* You
have seen enough. But this is the song
female anatomy sings, little one,
leaving you no choice

but to join in
and *love it, love it.*
No choice
but begin.

---

[2] Originally published in *Calyx, a journal of art and literature by women*, Volume 13, Number 2, Corvallis, Oregon, Summer 1991

The Hardness

Rick Bursky

When I was eight, my sister, sixteen,
pulled up her blouse and bra, and showed me
her breasts—petit white balloons with pink hats,
performers in an opera buffa as the curtain rises.
"You can look, but don't touch."
It was years before I realised
how perfect they were and that I had compared
them to every breast I'd seen since.
Eleven years later, I was a soldier in uniform,
a girl followed me into the men's room
at the bus station in Shreveport, Louisiana.
She wore a green shirt, jeans, short blond hair,
glasses too big for her face.
I washed my hands and ignored her.
When I turned to leave, she leaned back
against the door, pulled up her blouse and bra
and showed her breasts. "For ten dollars
you can touch them." There's a hardness
to the past the future will never know.
Two days of travel wrinkled my uniform.
I wanted to ask if she had done this before.
Is it the past or future that teaches us to pray?

The Underwear Thing

Janice A. Farringer

Chapel Hill, NC

My mother never discussed the facts of life with me. As a ten-year-old, I found a pamphlet left on my bedside table one day. Turning the pages in all directions, I puzzled over the drawings of male and female parts fitting into this or that via physiologically correct side-slice views complete with veins and arteries. It didn't make any sense to me, but I felt very grown up. Shortly thereafter, a giant blue box of Kotex napkins appeared on my closet shelf, and all my mother said was that I would need them one day soon. Huh?

Another thing that was never open to discussion with my mother was underwear. Completely not mentioned. If I needed underpants, I kind of had to hint broadly when we went on our annual back-to-school shopping expedition. One multi-pack of white cotton big pants a year seemed to be the limit. For back-to-school shopping, we always went to the same department store, down the stairs to the kids' clothes in the basement. I would pick stuff out, and my mother would reject them. I learned that it was easier just to nod at what she picked, go sullenly to the dressing room, and see how bad it was. Alone. One changed clothes alone. The one rule: always step into a dress, don't pull it over your head.

After I paraded a few dresses, my mother would say, "Do you want that one?" My response didn't really matter—all the dresses would be dreadful—but, since I got to say something, I tried to choose the least awful one. The only saving grace was that most of the time I was in Catholic school uniforms.

From this you may think we were strapped for cash or that working outside the home or something distracted my mother. Not so. She just didn't get the whole girly clothes thing, and she definitely didn't get my taste...or me in general. Eventually, I stopped going shopping with her at all. I wrangled a "clothing allowance" out of my parents then had to figure out how to dress well (by my standards) on practically nothing at all. What did I know about negotiating? I learned all about layaway, and I learned to sew really well.

Back to the underwear thing. Since it wasn't discussed, my white panties just were. I don't recall ever having prints or even pastel colours. Then I hit puberty, and I had these boob buds. We had to wear scratchy wool pleated skirts and white button-down shirts to school. There was not much chance for creativity. The nuns even forbade screw-backed dangly earrings. If any girl had shown up with pierced ears, there would have been a weeklong retreat on the spot to pray for guidance. But from fourth grade on, some of us started to acquire bras. Here was a real chance for creativity. You could see a bra through the back of a white cotton uniform shirt. If you could lay your hands on a colourful one...oh my, that would be great. Girls with bras became the object of envy and the occasional strap snapping.

Somewhere in there, my mother consented to my getting a training bra during our annual back-to-school shopping. I believe it was made out of some kind of stretchy white knit fabric—and had all the style of an Ace bandage. I wore it and hated it.

But I could say I had a bra.

When you are in throws of puberty, you sweat and you smell. I did the sweating part very well, and the smell followed. So I tried to keep my one bra clean and ready for wear. It was not easy. Apparently, my mother didn't think I needed one and therefore one was plenty. I was desperately trying to keep up appearances and trying not to stink.

I have to confess here that I was a good student in some respects and a lousy one in others. I could read up a storm and always tested four or five grades above grade level in reading, but for the life of me I could not spell. I memorised words for tests, but, if you randomly asked me how to spell something, you would likely get a mishmash of letters bearing little resemblance to the actual spelling of the word. I even had a spelling tutor during eighth grade because the nuns were convinced that this deficit in my learning would keep me from succeeding in high school. All this was pre-computer and pre-spellcheck, as you may have guessed.

One day my mother and I were driving around doing errands. We got near the once-a-year, back-to-school-shopping department store, and my heart quickened. Maybe we could go in there and get me another bra. So I said casually to her, "I need a B-A-R." No response. "Mother, I need a B-A-R," spelling it louder as if she were deaf.

She looked at me blankly. What was she thinking? My child wants to go to a bar in the middle of the day? My child? A bar? Is she a drinker?

Unable to communicate via this signal, I blurted out that I needed a bra.

It must have been a relief to her. I will never know. She pulled over to the parking lot by the department store, rifled in her purse, and handed me her store credit card.

"Okay," she said and reached over to the back seat for the book she kept in the car for reading through long carpool waits. She opened it and settled in, seemingly content.

I was mystified but got out of the car, clutching her card. I stumbled into the vast store and was hit by the cold air conditioning and the vast array of women's clothes on the first floor. No kids' area in the basement for me. I was going for the real thing. I tried to look sophisticated as I headed to the foundations department at the rear of the store. I would purchase a real bra. By myself.

For a while, I wandered among the boxes of Playtex Living Bras lined up under the plastic half mannequins. Giant double D's hung against the wall—suspended cotton slings that would fit no body I had ever seen. A sales woman finally asked me if she could help me.

I don't remember a thing after that. I must have gotten measured. I must have tried some bras on. I know I walked out of that department store with a padded bra to end all padded bras. It was so thick with foam rubber it could have stopped bullets. I had only aspirational boobs going in; now I had big honking bosoms. My mother never said a word.

I wore the bra to school the next day under my uniform shirt. I could only imagine what the nuns thought. Flat yesterday, Marilyn Monroe today. But it was white. It didn't show, and I was sure they had other things to worry about. I loved that bra. I tenderly washed it and wore it proudly for a couple years.

From that first padded statement, I progressed to more believable boob wear, even colourful ones and, best of all, black ones. But that lasting trauma at the end of childhood stayed with me. Having enough panties and bras has been a lifelong obsession. One of my favourite things to do even now is to go to an off-price chain store and flick thorough the sale underwear. I am drawn to leopard prints, wild stripes, and sweetly coloured cottons in equal measure. My bras are all fitted by professionals, though, at expensive boutiques that carry under-wires and push-ups, lace and sheer, nude and black, and everything in between.

My daughter can spell bra. She has loads of cute underwear I give her from those discount stores. She prefers to buy her bras all by herself, at Victoria's Secret. Ah, the circle of life.

To the Whiteness of Bone

Davi Walders

Caught between the future and the photographer's
eye, she is poised between protection and desire,
child and woman. White satin gathered tight over
stiff bone glints at the lens, cuts into cleavage.
Like pyramids in ancient light, triangles jut,
hiding, holding, rubbing against adolescent breasts.
The face half smiles, lips curved in contemplation
or longing for last night's good night kiss. Dark
lashes, pink flush upon cheeks, dewdrop pearls
peeking behind curls, she sits silent, almost
innocent, white gardenia cupped in hands curved
in her lap. A film of tulle, like a sprinkling
of talc, caresses bare shoulders, disappears
into organza billows below a nipped waist.

"Who needs a face (or was it brains) with boobs
like that?" Over and over, I heard it, bought it,
blushing and proud, stuffed the words deep like
Kleenex of the less well endowed. I learned my
lessons well, teasing in royal blue cashmere,
bartering in Rose Marie Reid sarongs, tutored
by rose-tipped fullness pulsing over an untaught
heart. Laughing at lockers, bending in search
of a chem book, dipping low to the Drifters,
I used them. On humid nights, plastic seats of pink
Ford convertibles, hair kinked, damp on steaming
necks; in winter dark, high above aching thighs,
sweating, pressed against the other, I used them.

Who knew about blue veins, milk stains on silk,
the scratch of an infant's nails, frenzy subsiding,

43

nipples turning brown and long from suckling,
La Leche women massaging more milk to stop the colic,
cold mammogram machines crushing soft tissue into
bruised purple, seeking reasons for immediate
removal? Who anticipated shoulder padded jackets,
herring bone suits hiding the dusky centers of
erogenous life, mid-level manager masquerades
reflected in glass ceilinged boardrooms, or the long,
slow descent of estrogen and gravity leveling all?

Searching the milky satin stretched tight across
the whiteness of bones, all I remember is a round
mirror above a ruffled vanity, the prom dress in mounds
on a bedroom floor, and a young woman bent, examining
scratches from unsealed seams, blood from the bite
of white tufts, red welts where bones carrying
valuable cargo dug into a twenty-four-inch waist, marking
the price of a 34D, dreaming of Saturday night.

Breast Imaging

Ann Cefola

In the bluest of rooms, I am awash in X-ray white.
My body's on lease to strangers:

Wrapped in paper, I mourn my lost topography,
my front yard with its swings and sandbox.

Around one breast a radiologist rolls metal in gel.
Traveling this ultrasound moonscape,

I see black pools pulse like tar pits.
She reassures, *just cysts.*

Poured into warm cotton held close,
my chaste white communicants

return to their warm-scented knit,
eyes like pink crocuses in snow,

roots delicate and lacy in red earth,
my certain garden, my creamy whole.

Curiosity Kills More Than Cats
J.M. Cornwell

Even as a small child, I was always curious and a little too observant, or so my parents thought.

My father was in the army, so we moved all over the country and even to Germany and Panama, so I was nearly six when I noticed my Aunt Edith's scar, which started next to her right arm and disappeared inside her sleeveless dress. "How did you get that?" I asked and pointed to the scar.

My mother grabbed my hand. "It's not polite to point or to ask questions like that."

Aunt Edith just smiled and said she had an operation. I didn't know what kind of operation until I was ten. Aunt Edith had a breast removed and wore a foam rubber pad that looked like a breast inside her bra so no one, except a very curious and observant child, would know it was gone. I didn't really understand what that had to do with me or what it all meant until November 2004, when I received a call from the clinic where I had undergone a mammogram six months before.

"We'd like you to have a repeat mammogram," the girl on the phone said. I wanted to know why. "There seems to have been a mix up with the records, and we need to redo the test."

"What kind of mix-up?"

"The doctor will discuss that with you."

I made an appointment. When I talked to the doctor, I learned my report had been misfiled and they needed to do a detailed mammogram and an ultrasound. I'd been through this before when I got my first mammogram eight years earlier and they found some lumps in both breasts. Remembering my aunt, I knew it wasn't the end of the world. Since I was also a medical transcriptionist and had typed hundreds of mastectomy results, I knew the options, and they didn't look all that bad. I could have an immediate breast reconstruction and new breasts with nipples that pointed up instead of farther down. I could live with those options until the doctor finished telling me the rest.

"The lumps look malignant, and there seems to be some spread to the lymph nodes."

My aunt popped back into my mind. She had lived a long time after her mastectomy, but she had waited too long. The cancer had already spread, and she died a prolonged and painful death. I had mammograms every year and had had them every six months after the benign cysts were discovered. Just eighteen months earlier, the cysts were gone and both breasts were clear, but now I was facing something much worse, something that should have been caught and dealt with seven months before. How had they missed it? Why had they waited so long to tell me?

"It looks like we can get you in next month," the doctor told me.

"Next month? How about this week or tomorrow?"

"They're booked up until next month."

My life was hanging in the balance, and he wanted me to wait another month. I couldn't believe what I heard.

The doctor calmly booked the appointment and handed me the slip of paper. I knew the possibilities and the dangers. I typed these reports every day. Every moment lost was another nail in my coffin, and there was nothing I could do about it.

More good news waited for me when I got home. My cousin, Mackie, Aunt Edith's oldest daughter, was dying. She had been diagnosed with breast cancer two years before and had both breasts removed—but not in time.

She had less than six months to live. I kept my news to myself. There was no sense in worrying my family when there was nothing they could do. They were in Ohio, and I was alone in Colorado. I'd tell them when there was something to tell.

I told a couple friends, but what would I do about John? We had just found each other, and now the future didn't look as rosy as we thought. I told him what the doctor told me and that it would be best if we didn't see each other anymore. Luckily, he lived three hours away, so it would be easy to break things off. I didn't look back. I focused on the test a few weeks away.

Openly frantic but understanding, John gave me some time, but he contacted my best friend and begged her to be there for me and to keep him informed (I wasn't talking to him and refused to see him). Christmas passed with a visit from an old friend and his partner. Then came the New Year, and the days counted slowly down. I agreed to see John but told him all bets were off if I had cancer.

The exam was on January 7th, and I would see John that afternoon after it was all over. My jaw ached from clenching as the technician centred the small plastic cone on different areas in the sides of my breasts. The ultrasound was easier and the technician much chattier. I was curious to see for myself what was happening inside my body, and she let me view the results on the black monitor. I didn't see anything, not even the little white circles I'd seen on my first ultrasound nearly nine years ago.

"I don't see anything," she said. "Your breasts are fine."

"What do you mean? I thought..."

"They're clear. No cysts or lumps or anything," she said. "Of course, the doctor will have to make the final determination, but I don't see anything suspicious."

I didn't know I'd been holding my breath until it

exploded from me in a wrenching sob. Another mistake, but this time it was in my favour. I couldn't wait to tell John.

The next day, John drove me up to Woodland Park to take the exams to get my amateur radio operator's license. I passed two of the three exams. One week later, I passed the third and took the final exam that made me an Extra with all frequency privileges. Things were looking better. I wouldn't get new breasts with nipples that pointed up instead of somewhere farther down, but I could keep the old ones and there would be no chemotherapy or radiation. I wanted to call my family to tell them the news and to let them know what I had been through the past two months, the good and the bad.

Before I could pick up the receiver, the phone rang. It was my mother. My cousin Mackie had died and been buried the week before. She had lived only two of the six months she thought she had. She died the day I found out I was all right.

We were both free of the cancer.

I never learned whose file the doctor's staff mixed up with mine. I could only pray she got her results or was curious enough to double check—no matter who it embarrassed.

Those Hands

Carol Dorf

This must be

the way men imagine desire.
Pillowed on my bare breast,
you sleep, one hand raised
defying gravity. Turning
to insistently nurse, hunger
returning. Your father tells you,
"It doesn't get any better."

We long for that all of our lives

Harriet says when I tell her,
(I'm tired, sore nipples, sore wrists)
you would be happiest
always attached to me,
sucking on the breast
almost as big as your head.

I feel

the Madonna with child
expression on my face
as you nurse. Sated, asleep,
you pull off. Milk drips
down one corner of your mouth.
Thumb and forefinger move
together and apart. Dream motion.
This I never imagined

before you arrived.

As you devour

my milk, the softness of hair,
scalp. Each time, at the beginning,
your hands bat at my breasts
then press into them.

The Great Christina

Christine Valentine

When I put on my sports bra
I am
The Great Christina
Musclewoman Extraordinaire

I am invincible
I have the strength of Atlas
The speed of cheetahs
The cunning of foxes
The claws of a grizzly

The Great Christina
Exercises for an hour
Takes off her sports bra
Normalizes
And vacuums the kitchen

Foreign Bras

Roberta Beach Jacobson

There's no book instructing a woman what to do when a parent dies 2500 miles away.

It was my job to travel across the Atlantic to the land of my birth to clean out my mom's belongings after she died. This was one journey in my life where I was completely alone. Being an only child, I had no siblings with whom to share the experience.

Part of the grieving process included the bittersweet task of going through her personal items. I had exactly twelve days in the house to get it all done. Then the family home in northern Illinois would be sold, the keys turned over to complete strangers who would know or care nothing about our family's celebrations by the fireplace or our Christmas dinners in the dining room. I understood before leaving Europe that I'd needed to pack a lifetime of memories into just a dozen days.

I was surprised to come across two dresser drawers full of nothing but bras.

What confronted me could have filled a brassiere museum. Why did Mom own so many bras? Some appeared to be practically antiques—my family heirlooms, representing every shade of almost-white, off-white, and could-have-once-been-white (something laundry soap advertisers would love to challenge them in a television commercial).

The bras probably spanned four decades, half my mother's life. Brassieres have gone through the evolution of concealing a woman's mammary glands completely to delightfully accenting them, lifting them as dangerously

high as possible—with little or no concern for comfort.
Basically, women get shaped into whatever society
dictates at the time. Thanks to the wonder of the
brassiere, breasts have probably gone through more
styling changes than any other part of the female
anatomy...the objective of which completely escapes me.

Maybe I scooted the grieving a few paces faster by
trying on Mom's assortment of bras. What I was saying
was, "I accept you're gone, but you're not forgotten." Our
generation gap was clear. Where I could term bras as
optional apparel, my mother's generation celebrated a
sense of freedom once they stopped wearing bras to bed
under their pyjamas.

The idea of not wearing a bra during daylight hours
would have never occurred to her. A bra was part of the
female experience, a given. I remembered Mom dressed
in a fine tweed dress, down on her hands and knees,
scrubbing the kitchen floor. In fact, she only dared to
buy her first slacks in the early 1970s. (Of course, she
wore pantyhose underneath, because that's how a lady
dressed, she explained to me.)

After days of cleaning and sorting, selling some
furniture and filling box after box of items to go to
charitable organisations, I locked up my childhood home
for the last time. The taxi was waiting. The driver loaded
my unmatched suitcases (bras inside folded neatly—cup
over cup, as Mom had patiently taught me to do with my
training bras when I was eleven), and we headed to the
airport.

I'd like to tell you that, when I landed in Frankfurt,
Germany, customs inspectors opened my suitcases and
gasped at all the foreign bras, but that's not how this
story ends.

Customs, for once in my traveling life, just waved me
through. I even got half a smile.

Maybe they knew.

Soundings

Sarah Conover

Nothing brought us together but the food
on the table. Six lives drifting.
I stared at the place mat, a nautical chart,
my dinner plate afloat over the varying depths
of hidden sea floor as it glided from Montauk
to Greenwich, avoiding the shoals of single digits.
I knew to keep quiet and plot my course away
from here, across Long Island Sound, out to sea.
But Dad had already downed two martinis,
and his old anger leaked its brine
around us, encircling and threatening.
You could count on its daily rising, like a tide.
The table settings never varied, the shorelines
on the maps remained fixed, but we girls changed.
A breast man himself, he named all of ours after foods—
watermelons, cookies, raisins.
I tried to submarine down, under the table.
When I finally could slip away from
the room, he noticed my ass. Many men
are ass men, don't worry he said.
After that, a chart he had sounded with his eyes,
my body was never my own.
In the mirror, I saw what he saw:
a shallow stinginess when I faced
myself full on, and no way to see
from behind, where he said
I was beautiful.

The Bra Poem

Andrea Potos

To the prize-winning poet who says
she's tired of poetry where women wax sentimental
about birthing, mothering,
worn subjects like menopause and menarche:

You won't want to hear how, in junior high,
I'd press my nipples in and out like tiny
collapsed balloons, waiting for them to fill.
How I yearned for graduation
from my cotton half-undershirt
to a padded bra with real hooks and eyes
my girlfriends could snap
when they snuck behind me.
It won't matter to you how,
the morning my mother and I returned
from Gimbels lingerie,
I pulled my best friend Cassie into the back yard
and in between the sheets drying on the line;
how I flung off my shirt for her, like a sculptor
unveiling the masterpiece it has taken her
twelve years to create—breasts
the color of sun-braised daffodils,
two cups to hold
my double A treasure.

Anatomy of My Clogged Duct

Sarah Werthan Buttenwieser

That morning, my right breast hurt. Had Remy been suckling extra hard due to his cough? Had his burgeoning new teeth scraped me? My hand floated up to my engorged breast. I pressed my fingers against a small hard plane.

Working backward, I recalled the cold that racked me with a constant cough and quicksand grade fatigue, preceded by the sore throat, preceded by the loss of my voice after a sleepless night, which began when the phone rang at eleven.

"Wendy's waters broke," Arlene announced. "The babies will be out within half an hour."

Wendy was the gestational surrogate Arlene and her husband had contracted to carry twins. Although I'd spent a long time mulling the strange science fictional dimensions of the situation, I had not considered the possibility that, with an emergency caesarean section, the intended parents would miss the birth.

Remy woke up at eleven-thirty, one and three something—a newborn night, although he was nearly eight months old. Wendy's pregnancy had reached just twenty-nine weeks.

At four fifty-one, Arlene called again. Her voice sounded at once shaky and flat. "They're under two-and-a-half pounds each. Baby A is showing signs of respiratory distress." Arlene had worried before every test and every ultrasound then sounded exultant at every perfect score. "Can you look up Respiratory Distress Syndrome?" she asked. "I'll call you back later."

Within forty-five minutes, I learned that Respiratory Distress Syndrome is a complication due to immature lungs and that some babies also experience Bronchopulmonary Dysplasia, meaning they have trouble weaning from the respirator. I high-tailed it off the Internet, that big black hole of illness.[3] Potential horrors mattered little without a specific diagnosis, I decided, the most clearheaded thought I had in that hour between five and six. I watched the sky peel away darkness and daylight usher itself in without fanfare. I felt sad and empty and scared; Arlene so wanted a baby...babies...and she so wanted the experience to be perfect. This wasn't perfect, that much was certain.

By the time Arlene rang back, I'd rehearsed my speech; without knowing enough about Baby A's condition, it was impossible to discover anything definitive about RSD on the Internet.

Instead, Arlene began, "I can't believe this isn't working out the way it's supposed to. Wendy had five full-term children naturally. She was supposed to deliver perfectly healthy babies."

Arlene endured infertility's rigmaroles for years: waiting, acupuncture, positive thinking, drugs, in-vitro fertilisation (plural), and miscarriage (also plural). Because of questionable egg quality and quantity, her doctors warned against another pregnancy attempt, leaving her with two options: find a gestational surrogate or pursue adoption. Without a moment's hesitation, she and her husband opted for the surrogate. After matching with Wendy, a protracted struggle to retrieve eggs ensured. Eventually, two took: a boy and a girl.

"I know. I know," I offered, hesitatingly. "But parenthood, so much of it, is out of our hands."

As far as I was concerned, my old friend had been taken hostage by infertility. Skeptical about the use of hormones, she'd been unwilling to consider the pill back

---

[3] With thanks to Nancy Gonter

when she assumed she was fertile, but, ever since her infertility began, she'd taken hormones orally and via injection without once questioning safety or efficacy. Before we had kids, in our twenties, we'd attended abortion rights rallies together. Although she hadn't exactly waffled about this politically, any rejection of a pregnancy had become unbearable. And children made her cry. "I hate seeing them in the supermarket," she confessed numerous times. I tried to call only when she wouldn't hear mine. Meanwhile, she and her husband sank their savings into theoretical babies.

"We did everything," she pleaded, sniffling.

I replied, "You kind of deal with what is, not what you want it to be."

The pain of a clogged milk duct is unyielding.

"Maybe I have breast cancer," I whispered to my husband.

Alien invasion: a stone appears from nowhere beneath the skin. First merely hard, after a few hours the lump heats up, a feverish and rigid entity inside your body, barely visible at skin level. Breasts are not polite body parts to touch in public.

Remy banged an empty plastic cup in close orbit to my body. As the object hit my breast, a jagged stone to my body, I leapt.

And the baby, who had already claimed the breasts, continued to nurse. Pain spit in fiery blasts. Feeding him was my potential salvation; his mighty, incising mouth, designed for sucking, might undo the damage. Each time he wanted to nurse, I pulled him close, breathed extra hard, and closed my eyes until the pain subsided, waiting for sweet relief. But the baby's sucking did nothing to crumble the rocky ridge of stopped-up milk. I swung him around to the easy side. My hand returned to the tender area. Hope leeched away. By the time darkness fell, the spot had grown larger, hotter, and more painful, unyielding.

That I had started having trouble at a primary source of nurturing made sense, having sat with my own ambivalence for so long. It had seemed as if the best way to be Arlene's friend throughout her infertility ordeal had been to hold my tongue.

From Arlene's point of view, my having children rendered me unable to empathise (likely true). Although my list of concerns was as long as a grocery list, my major uneasiness centred upon one thing. So much went into garnering what began to seem closer to ownership than blood relation, involving so much suffering, so many physical and financial resources, so many health risks, and so many other people. All of this effort was expended in order to reach parenthood's starting line, the laundry and the endless nights and the complete surrender. It would be weeks before Arlene's babies went home. Arlene was beginning to realise she'd be watching for developmental delays and hoping for respiratory health. She was letting go of anticipated perfection, heading toward reality. At the same time, these were her choices, and she had every right to make them. If I defended the right to choose not to have a child for every woman, I must also support her right to try—as she, not I, deemed reasonable—to have one.

My paltry efforts to remedy the clogged duct that day—I dashed in and out of hot showers, slapped a couple of hot compresses on the lump, and spent five minutes on the breast pump—accomplished nothing. Late that evening, within a ninety-minute period, I went from hot compress to the pump then hot shower to hot compress to a return to the pump. The underside of the duct deflated a tiny bit, but the mass above the nipple remained lodged there, bigger, blisteringly hot, and inert.

Slightly damp, exhausted, wholly defeated, I gave up; I would sleep and try to undo the damage in the morning. The baby cried out. The last thing I wanted to do was feed him, but, dutifully, I pulled him from his crib. We settled on my bed. I drew him to the painful breast. He began to suck then to suck more eagerly at double the usual speed. "I think you've got it, baby," I whispered as I watched him chomp away with the enthusiasm of a cartoon character in action. Gingerly, I lifted my hand to the sore spot. No longer a stiff fortress...broken, soft again, cooler already...I had my breast back. "Thank you," I told the baby boy. "I love you."

Milk gland as location of my sadness...that also fits. The experience of breastfeeding my children has been one of my greatest pleasures. Beholden to formula to supplement breast milk for my first child, I am neither a purist nor a breastfeeding zealot. Bottle-feeding works better for many people, for as many reasons. Yet having now been, three times over, someone's source of nourishment and unique comfort, I remain awed by the way those functions become intertwined, revere the web of our entanglements. I don't want to wax poetic or anti-feminist here; breastfeeding has been my privilege and my pleasure. This third baby, who spit up profusely for months, has never taken a bottle. To be tethered to him in the bustling household—three kids, two working parents—has been a gift. The constancy with which I must return has rendered leaving him easy, freed me to focus on the bigger children and my own work. That tender spot with its junky build-up—so obvious in its placement—allowed me to locate my own sadness. Although the delineation was pre-ordained in the case of this surrogate and intended parent relationship, I ached at the thought of a woman with milk in her breasts an hour from the babies and another with two bottles in her hands in order to feed the twins. I couldn't help wondering about Wendy, identifying with her to whatever degree.

What is patently obvious is that the making of families and unfolding of families are complicated matters. Unlike a clogged milk duct, which does dissolve and resolve, dynamics in a family remain murkier and less easily understood. Even if endlessly discussed, there's no definitive answer, like the whole debate about whether breastfeeding is all that important. How crucial are those nutrients and antibodies? Must breastfeeding tie mother and child together in a connection both strong and delicate at once, like a spider's filaments of silk? Those shimmering and sturdy bonds can be created in other ways. As families, we are woven together by birth, love, and even technology. We continue spinning once we are part of the pattern: for dear life.

The Bammo Mammo

Wendy Buffington

Breast pressed flat,
impressed, depressed,

Do you take hormone replacements?
No. Do you take American Express?

Rolled like dough—Whoa!
A hard-boiled egg? You don't say.

Sonogram, candygram:
Hope you're feeling better, ma'am,

and I am, though my sweater falls flat
on the left, cleavage

uncleaved, bra unfilled, an empty
sleeve, bereft of the breast that lived

in its pocket, this flap of skin
a souvenir like a lock of hair

from the dead saved in a locket,
instead of that big girl, Tilt-a-Whirl

one-eyed monster, O googly-eyed wonder
who used to live there—

But I don't miss her much so far,
I have her stare tattooed

across this puckered scar.

Date with a Mammo

Linda Simone

Steely cold lover-artist, you splay
your arms, take me—one
of many—in crushing embrace.

Your red eye pricks
my naked breasts.
Voyeurs run for cover.

My breath stops. I
barely hear your moan.
You are done.

You capture me—
chiaroscuro—
on your black canvas.

And no matter how sweet,
how bitter your words,
you know I will return.

My Mother's Nipples

Maria Nazos

—after Bob Haas

I remember them: freakishly large, pink nubbins, and the way she would swath a towel around her head and step naked from the shower—

Concave stomach, lower abdominal slope, the wiry black grove of pubic growth. I remember my mother's nipples not when it mattered, not when I bit the breast that fed me, not until years later.

An ancient Greek myth my mother read to me as a child: Hercules was being breastfed by Hera. Unbeknownst to her, he was the product of one of her philandering husband's many affairs, and she didn't recognise him as the same child who crushed two white vipers she'd sent out to kill him upon his birth.

And the way my mother looked up at this point in the story. "Now don't get the idea that Hera likes baby Hercules," she said. "She doesn't. She's just breastfeeding him."

Back to the story: Hercules bit down on Hera's nipple, sending her spray exploding across the sky, where it stayed. This was how the Milky Way came to be.

Those years we lived in Greece, the house was marble encased by a white balcony, and it was white, all white, in fact, with gargantuan columns. The yard was dirt with a single palm in the middle and cumquat trees and figs bursting with mealy fecundity—the same bruised, purple inside as a nipple. And the yard smelled of a hundred bleating, breeding tomcats. My mother was wild with loathing for the cats. She would stand outside, at the top of the marble stairs that glinted in the sun, and hiss and stomp until the cats would scatter like terrified krill under rocks. She refused to drive or walk outside of the house because she claimed she once saw a naked man in the bushes on the way to the kiosk to buy cigarettes.

She was always calling her aging mother in Illinois and crying that she wanted to leave this place.

Nights, she and my aunt would go to wild carnival parties; I saw the photos of my aunt dressed as a hula dancer with bare shoulders and a pair of plastic breasts, topped with hard nipples. She was sitting with my mother, who told me that, at the last minute, she put on a white puffy wig she brought along and borrowed my aunt's mascara to paint large, black spots on her face right before a woman at the party got on a glass table to dance and fell over. "They were beauty marks," she explained.

The first woman's nipples I had ever felt, except my own: Annie Marino's, eight years ago in Southern Illinois, where we moved after my mother's mother fell ill. I asked Annie what she'd like me to do. She refused to answer. I recall the way she felt, the way they felt: like two hard little knots, two stubborn buds that refused to break through to the surface, that withheld their secret and kept you guessing at the beauty they might contain.

In 1967, my mother left Northwestern University. Whether she dropped out or was kicked out is unknown. All I have managed to derive from my mother's early adulthood is from the beautifully-slurred words of drunken relatives at family parties.

"She went to Greenwich Village with three blacks," Aunt Connie said. "Three black panthers, I remember.

She was calling her mother every hour to check in. God knows what would have happened, had her mother found out! She was in love with one of them, one of the blacks." My aunt leaned in. Her glasses magnified her eyes until they looked as big as twin dinner plates and, under the lenses, just as glossy. "Shhhhh...never repeat this..."

When we moved to the US, which, all this time, my mother so adamantly said she wanted to do, and left my father in Greece to captain boats, she would often sit in our new house in Joliet, Illinois, and drink tumblers of vodka in the plaid living room. The big house we bought—that she said she'd always wanted—seemed to loom even larger around her, in her seashell-pink bathrobe on the couch. Often the bathrobe drooped, revealing one brown nipple; her breasts hung lower than I remembered. Often she would drink until her face flushed, excited and feverish. Sometimes she would tell me it was all my fault, the fact that she was self-destructing, because I never helped clean up the house, and the house was dirty, dirty. Then she would get some Clorox, dump it in a bucket, and start cleaning the floor. Every night, I felt something inside me break and break down. Usually I would yell back. I would curse until the words flew out of my mouth like black moths. Mostly, though, she would sit on the couch and drink.

The first man who ever saw my nipples was Andy Madonis. Eleventh grade. On the floor of a friend's empty rented or recently moved into apartment in Joliet, Illinois. I told Adrianne, a friend more experienced than I.

"Isn't it great?" she said and shook my hand. She would later drop out of school, go on to become addicted to heroin then suddenly clean up and win a TV modeling show. She went on to pose for *Playboy*, and, years later, I saw her—splayed naked on a cream-coloured floor, her legs longer and more tragically beautiful than a Russian novel, laced with gold high heels that rested against a gilded couch. The first woman to hear about my first nipple-play—more intimate than when Andy first saw them.

Years later, I ran off to Cape Cod and worked at a dessert café. The owner's wife made chocolate replicas of bodily appendages. My gay friend, Mark, who worked with me, took one look at a breast lollipop—bright white with a nipple in the centre, bright fuchsia like the stamen of a flower—and sneered.

"Nipples are not that colour," he said.

"Yes, they are," I said. "They can be, I mean. I promise. They can be different colours according to, you know, arousal."

"Not that colour, though."

Behind the barista station, I pulled down the front of my blouse to expose my left breast. "See? Mine are a coffee colour. All different colours."

Mark almost fainted. "I see," he finally said.

I used to watch my mother put on makeup before going to a party in Greece. She would make her face pale with foundation. ("In my day, it was considered elegant to be pale.") Then she would dot her face with burnt sienna lipstick and rubbed it in. My favourite part? The way she held her hand steady and drew a freehand, blue-black line across her eyelid. She had to be the most beautiful woman in the world.

One night, I was lying in bed, and it was one of those nights; I had to be one of the only people left awake in the world, and my mother came into my room. She was usually drunk at this time, but, for once, she was sober. She came over to the edge of my bed. "Mind if I sit here?" And perched at the edge of it for a minute. Her frame was small in her pink robe, but she sat very tall, very straight. For once, she didn't sway as if blown by some imaginary breeze. She was quiet and sat for a long while. The night, it seemed, sat quiet and long also. The moon washed her features silver.

For some reason, this is all I return to. She seems lonely but strong. It is the scene that never begins and never ends. Somewhere in time, the mother is sitting at the edge of her daughter's bed, and the transition is not a transition but a moment in which the ego drops away and a person reveals themselves beyond the struggle with diction. This is all I have. All I return to.

The Oracles

Ruth Bavetta

The first doctor
has a fine head of white hair.
He says the only cure
is to cut it all off.
But first he will need
an x-ray of my chest,
a chart of my heart.

The second doctor says
it's up to me. He can take
the entire breast, or a portion,
whichever I want.
What I want is to run
from the room.

Doctor number three
bounds into the room
in purple pants and tennis shoes.
The good news, he says,
is that I do not have cancer.
Then he reads the pathology report
again. Oops, he didn't see that part.
But never fear, the lumpectomist
is here.

The last doctor looks younger
than my youngest son, smiles,
sits down, asks how I'm feeling.
Lumpectomy is the way to go,

and can he please,
for his research,
have a piece of my breast
and a *soupçon* of blood?

Dreams of a Good Prognosis

Daisy Levy

Your scar is my own,
raspberry red and long.
I look down at my chest,
see one nipple,
one neat slice
across my body, down
to the armpit. Here.
Touch this.

Mammograms and Mielie-Pitte

Kerry-lyn Radloff

Some years ago I returned home to South Africa, convinced I had skills and experience to offer after all! I had been in New Zealand for a time, seriously considering immigration, when this revelation came to me. One year after that, I was still unemployed, had exhausted any funds I had brought home with me in trying to keep my two girls and I together, and was possessed of a lump or two in my left breast.

Undaunted, I remembered one could—in the good old days before people (myself included, although I had come back, so surely that exonerated me somewhat) started jumping ship in the wake of our new elections—make use of State facilities, and so I hove off in October of that year to Grey's State Hospital, optimistic that there my lumpiness would be sorted out. No one warned me—take a book!

Take *War and Peace. The Lord of the Rings*! An hour after arriving, I was given a white card and shown, ever so nicely, down the passage to the Place Where It Would All Be Sorted Out. Four and a half hours later, I was on the base of my spine in an uncompromising plastic chair, behaving like a two-year-old! I rolled and I heaved, I pleaded and I bargained, but nothing could make things happen—albeit those Sisters were charming. Charming and implacable. Immovable. Your turn will come, they insisted. I *knew* that—but when?

For a time I amused myself with my fellow two-year-olds—although I steered a wide berth around the amputee and the coughee; I just couldn't bring myself to study them too closely. I did find it fun (for a while) playing musical chairs with an incredibly smelly old man who kept insisting that those Sisters bring air freshener and spray the room. We all smelled quite horrible, he said, often and loudly. I tried chatting with one or two equally desperate looking women, but missing teeth and missing vocab between us wasn't exactly making for polite conversation. I was too afraid of losing my place to go outside and have a look to see whether the world was exactly as I had left it eons before—and was practically on the verge of believing, after all those hours passed, that I might well be able to class myself as a Missing Person from now on. Finally! My turn.

A most pleasant Indian doctor smiled sweetly at me as he stuck a needle into the most promising lump, sucked out whatever it was he was aiming for, handed me a tissue to mop the sudden tears I leaked at my plight, and told me to come back in two weeks for results. Two weeks! To go through all this waiting again? I don't know!

Anyway, two weeks later, book in hand, I was back at Grey's (I'd gained experience, you see). Five hours later (and I only managed half the book, too!) I was again sweetly smiled at, told tests were inconclusive, and would I please have a mammogram. No problem! Show me the way, I said. And so I was. All the way down to a small office, somewhere near the entrance, from which a lovely lady booked me an appointment...at Edendale State—on the other side of the city! Well, I couldn't very well walk right now, could I? Which was just as well, as the nearest date was for January.

Fuming just a little, I went off to sulk over Christmas, and January came, as it will. My car had been reversed into and thus had no window and practically no door (and was likely to stay that way given my unemployed and uninsured current state of being!)—so I borrowed my mother's for my epic journey to Edendale. Having never been there, I asked directions of a friend and was told it was easy to find—just watch out for the sign.

I watched. I saw it. I drove straight past it, as well—and trundled off down the road towards the township, dodging taxis filled with every possible rapist and hijacker in South Africa—and swearing like an out-of-work trucker. I slipped my sunglasses off my nose and hid them in the cubby hole as I was driving. Rolled up the windows and locked all the doors. I mean, here I was, driving off into the great unknown, and a huge concrete wall separated me from the road back—I was a mite anxious! All the stuff one read of rape and carnage in this country of mine, and here I was providing the very next statistic! I eventually managed to avoid several oncoming taxis and rolled the car through a caved-in gap in the concrete wall, over the verge and onto the road back towards where I ought to have been in the first place and got myself to Edendale Hospital without further mishap. Smug, I negotiated a parking, locked the car, and sauntered off to find where I could get this sodding mammogram done.

Finding the admissions desk was a breeze—someone had ever so conveniently left a trail of (dried) bloody footprints all along the linoleum for me to follow. Sweating a little and starting to feel somewhat out of my depth, if not a little bilious, I found the desk and was ushered towards the back stairs to the second floor. Strict instructions where given me *not* to use the lifts, as they didn't work properly, so I climbed stairs where I was told to climb and delicately (holding my breath against god knows what!) stepped around boxes of unidentifiable and quite possibly ghastly contents and brooms and bits of discarded cotton wool to find where I had to be. I was still confident at this stage. I had an appointment, after all, and I was most timeous, notwithstanding my jaunt on the road.

I informed the nurse behind the grill that I was there for my 8:30 A.M. appointment and was politely asked to sit "over there." So I did. For two hours. More two-year-old behaviour, which earned me little more than ever increasing impatience until, finally, unable to contain myself—and convinced by now, too, that these people here knew something about my left breast that I didn't and just weren't telling me, which was why they were stalling so much—I slammed most grumpily to the desk at the grill for the umpteenth time and demanded I see the Most Important Person there.

Granted, despite my ugly scowl and my singular sense of humour failure, they were polite as they ushered the Most Important Person in my general direction. Listen here, I said, trying to be equally sanguine, I have been waiting two sodding hours for my 8:30 appointment for a mammogram, which process began over two bloody months ago. Are you going to let me sit here with my breast malignifying, or are you going to do the deed? There, I thought, this ought to get them going! And it did.

Madam, I was told...Madam, we are most sorry, but the machine? The mammogram machine? She is fucked.

There we go then. The machine, she is fucked.

Out of the mouth of the Most Important Mammogram-Taking Person there. Verbatim!

What can a left breast do? It goes home with promises that it will be called and will be the *very* first one pressed between glass once the machine is fixed. Three weeks later, during which time I had very seriously considered asking a friend to back his car out of his garage, allow me to lie myself down on the floor of it then have him gently drive the rear tyre of his vehicle over my delicately exposed left breast, thus pressing it as flat as the missing mammogram required—at least I would have the satisfaction of being able to relate to all other mammo victims, even if I never managed to actually have one done, which, given the rate things in my non-Medical Aid state were going, seemed unlikely—I was phoned, told the machine, she is now working, please be here tomorrow by 9 A.M. sharp! And you will be our first patient of the day!

Excellent! I didn't even bother to take my book!

Pity!

Three hours later...

A man walked down the corridor and sat right next to me on the bench reserved for mammo patients. I was prepared to be indulgent, as I was desperately in need of something with which to occupy my calcifying mind. There had to be some plausible reason for his sitting there. He had wild knotty hair and a bag of *mielie-pitte* that he laid on the floor between his feet as he made signs of a vague and somewhat demented cross in the air around him. This done, he sat back, leaned on me, and extracted from his trouser pocket a piece of newspaper and a baggie. He rolled himself a joint with aplomb; then, leaning down, he took his left foot out of his shoe and put the joint into it for safe keeping. It was at that point that I noticed his foot was neatly wrapped in a stunning pair of purple knickers, complete with lace. Lovely! From mammo to mental in one move!

He thereupon removed a pen from the depths of his hair and began writing god alone knows what all over the thigh of his trousers, interspersed with rapid hand movements in the air around him and the odd crotch scratch.

He wrote and he wrote; when he began to eye my trouser leg with artistic avarice, I lay forward on my legs with my arms dangling to the floor and watched him through my hair. I was too scared, dammit, to move in case that mammo got away from me! And I was not letting this man draw on the blank canvas of my blue jeans, either, even if it was decidedly unchristian of me to be so terribly selfish. There was a limit to the poetic licence one could allow, notwithstanding the circumstances. Also, I was transfixed by this *mielie-pitte* maniac!

He tired, apparently, of writing and gesticulating. Taking up his joint, he put his pantied foot back into his shoe, stood up, and spoke directly to me. I affected complete neural failure until my neighbour on the other side translated and told me this man wanted me to watch his *mielie-pitte* whilst he went outside. Okay! No problem. I can watch pips for my country! I watched and I watched. At least it gave me something constructive to do.

Some twenty minutes later he returned and came and stood right in front of me. He gazed at me for what seemed ages. He made a sign of the cross in the air between us. Then, with remarkable agility, he began to leap up and down all over that bag of *mielies*, screaming They're moving! They're moving! as *mealie-pitte* shot in every which direction along that corridor.

I left. I admit it. I just left. I gave up the good fight and went home.

It's a year later, and my breast is exactly where I had it last—attached to my chest. I don't care if they call me every day for a month, offering me a car, a trip to the moon, and a job as Personal Assistant to the President if I come along to be the first patient—I am *not* going!

Benign Hope

Jenni L. Ivins

They removed the lump
but left a hole
where fear sometimes seeps.
Is it really gone?
What else will grow?
Am I paranoid?
How can I know?

My bras don't fit
entirely
though one cup fits okay.
When the right cup is right
the left overflows
and when the left one fits
the right wrinkles and folds.
Like a hopeful adolescent
I bolster with tissues
and no one knows but me.

However
I'm known not by my chest
but by my heart.
My love, my laughter and my deeds
should all be more prominent
for I am alive!
I can love, laugh and do deeds.
I am fortunate.

As grave as my fears may be—

my grave is just an empty hole
where no malignancy lies.

Double D Auntie

Rose Hammond

My nephew will turn eighteen very soon. From the first time I saw him in the incubator at the hospital, I knew we would share a special bond during our lifetimes. When I was later asked to be his godmother, I had to admit that, despite feeling very close to him, I was surprised that my sister chose me. I was the only member of my family who did not have children, I was still a party girl, and my maternal instincts at that time of my life were non-existent.

As a baby, my nephew was a cuddler. He loved to lie on my breasts and fall asleep. Sometimes, we would watch videos together or just sit quietly while I read his little books to him. When he grew taller than me, which didn't take very long, he would pout and bend down to feign placing his head on my breast when he wanted something, most likely something his mom refused to buy him. I usually caved in to his requests.

It's probably worth mentioning that my four sisters and our mother are all B cups, and I am the only one who wears a double D. I've been told that I have my grandmother's breasts.

Throughout my nephew's formative years, I evolved into "Auntie," the backup "Mom" who gave great presents on birthdays and holidays, took him shopping, drove him places, acted as confidant, spoke his language, and acted as a buffer when my sister became too much for him to handle. After all, I was "Auntie."

Our family, although close, had its ups and downs like most families. During one particular year, we all seemed to be in free fall. My nephew, who was becoming a young man, had developed some inner struggles and somehow became distant from me. Having my nephew express his dislike of me wounded me in a way that I had never experienced before. I had lost friends and boyfriends, but the pain never equated to that.

We did eventually reconcile our differences, and we now have a more adult relationship that sometimes regresses, but I don't mind.

My breasts never seemed to be a source of pride but rather of exhibition; people noticed my breasts before they noticed me. I never wanted to be different, at least not like that. After decades as a double D, I've recently decided to have my breasts reduced and am awaiting a consultation with the plastic surgeon.

My family has been very supportive of my decision and has assured me that I am going to feel so much better once I have the operation. I believe I will be fine, physically, but psychologically, am I going to mourn my most defining feature?

Interestingly enough, my nephew was the only family member who spoke out against my operation. His only comment was, "Where will I lay my head when I need comfort?"

A Well Set Table

Georgia A. Greeley

I was somewhere between
the ages of four and six when
my mother realised, if she wanted
a well set table, she should ask me.

I was the only one of five children
who would take the time to match
the multiple flatware patterns, space the dishes and
glasses just so, or line up the place
settings across from each other
on our grey-flecked Formica kitchen table.

So it made sense to me
when I had cancer in one breast
to have the surgeon cut off both.
Who would want only one breast?
I would no longer match,
my body would somehow lose
its powerful, symmetrical balance.
I thought I had chosen control.

I never realised how much I'd miss nipples,
with their irritating little sphincter muscles
which give away so much;
how cold it is,
whether or not you're wearing a bra,
that yes your body is aroused—
even though your mind is still writing poems—dammit.

I'm setting the table for my grandsons today,
two lovely, rowdy boys with uncombed curls.
I still match the flatware, space the dishes,
set the glasses just so. I decide we're going
to eat dessert first, set the last course at each place setting,
and notice each sweet dollop of whipped cream
nippling the round mounds of Jell-O.

The Package
Martha Witt

Having set a lovely silver lamp on the wooden dining room table, Celia invited her husband to sit—a candle would have been overly sentimental, an exaggeration. She was too expert for that.

"Tell me something you have never told me before," she proposed. "And then I will do the same." It took Domenico an entire minute to seat himself at the table. A man who had been agile and quick as a cat—she had only recently begun to believe the doctor's dire predictions; otherwise, she never would have proposed this game. When he was finally seated, he watched her another full minute before taking off his glasses and dropping them on the table with a small plink. The skin beneath his eyes was puffy and vulnerable in the lamplight, so she was half inclined to advise him to move farther back into the shadows. "Are you comfortable?"

"Yes." His hair, though no longer black, lay smoothed against his head as always, inspiring in her a pang of gratitude. Despite his illness, Domenico went through the routine of his toilette every morning, saving his hair for last. With a little gel in his comb, he brushed it back, surveying his movements carefully in the mirror, overseeing a procedure far more complex than merely combing hair. Back in the early days of living together, when they still made love, he would allow her to touch his hair.

She wished to touch his hair once again that evening, before beginning the game. Celia actually clasped her hands together in order to suppress her desire.

93

"What are we doing?" he asked, looking around the room, past her, towards the darkness. He was old, Dio mio—eighty-one years old! In her childhood, she had never known anyone so old. "Well?" He leaned forward, surprisingly willing.

She shrugged, and her smile was for him, generated to appease, not a reflection of her inner state.

He blinked, breathed through his nostrils, and twisted his left cufflink into place. He owned beautiful shirts. Despite his illness, he dressed well every evening, as he always had. Domenico was a lover of fine things, appreciating their weight and texture. How often she had seen him hold an expensive object, close his eyes, and tell the salesman a few minutes later that it was not worth half what he was asking for it. On the other hand, there were little silver boxes or thick wooden frames that others overlooked and for which he would have paid more dearly than the price tag required.

As long as she could remember, in fact, he owned a small square made of twenty-four-karat gold. He had bought the gold from a dentist and had paid a jeweller to form it into a perfect square, which he let no one else touch because he claimed the gold was so pure that it was still malleable. He kept the square handy for times when his patience wore thin, which it often did when he was with her. In fact, he extracted it from his pocket as she explained the game to him, and he held it pressed into the palm of his hand.

"Do you understand the rules?" she asked, wishing he would focus on her now, for God's sake.

He had once promised her that anyone could appreciate a beautiful lady when she was young and in full bloom, but that his rare talent was the ability to value true beauty—the quality of skin, hair, and bone structure—in women long past youth. "There are plenty of pretty women in their twenties," he had told her, "but only the genuine beauties endure, and it takes a trained eye to spot the real thing early on." He had promised her all this long ago in a single breath. "You are the real thing."

"Shall we play?" she asked.

"Yes." His old schoolmaster yes, a final note cutting short any further discussion: Si'.

"Fine, then." She looked at him. "I never told you that I take English lessons. I have been taking English lessons for five years now." She tried to sound reasonable, practical. "I always thought I'd go to America if you left me, to New York City."

"Where were you taking lessons?" he asked, quietly settling his eyes on her face.

"I had a tutor come to the house."

He gave a nod.

She'd been so careful, had instructed Soccorro never to mention anything, had cancelled her lesson when she thought he'd be home early. But now that her secret was out, she realised she'd wasted her energy. He had no more questions.

"I suppose you are waiting for me to confess something you've known for years. Do you really want me to say it? Will it even count," he asked, "in terms of our game?" He pressed the tips of his fingers together to form a triangle and rested his lips on the apex. He smiled, angling his head slightly, as though indulging a mere girl.

Celia straightened. "Yes. Go ahead."

"Ah." Domenico raised his eyebrows, placing her squarely in his line of vision as one whose discipline required a firm, constant hand. "Why a confession?" His eyes finally fixed on hers.

"She died, didn't she?"

According to his own, unspoken rule, Domenico waited almost a full minute before speaking. "You have always had a lovely face."

Celia produced a slight laugh, more like a wheeze. It

had been so long since she had flirted that she feared he might simply get up and leave.

To her surprise, Domenico covered her hands, picked them up, and held them to his lips then returned them to the table. "I am heartbroken," he confessed, observing her fingertips.

Tears stung her eyes, but she did not cry.

"Now he is dead," Dona Celia states out loud in English. It is a simple sentence, the kind to be sent by telegram, a solid piece of information. Celia would not mind if there were more sentences as weighted and uncomplicated as this one. It is true that part of her fascination with the English language is due to its simplicity and the informative subject-verb-object structure of most sentences. Subject-verb-predicate-adjective, in this case. She might add, "He died three days ago. He was eighty-one."

Celia need never again put down her cup of coffee to greet the nurse, who entered precisely at eight with her aerobic smile and "Bom dia!" She will never again go to the room to check on Domenico after lunch and before settling down for her nap.

Though the disease had been in his pancreas, the doctors had said something about heart failure. She was sure, of course, his physical heart was peripheral to the matter. Domenico had spent the last six months drifting in and out of consciousness, and before that he had been so sullen and listless that there would be days wherein they exchanged less than a sentence with each other. Not that he had ever spoken to her much. Nonetheless, his presence provided a rhythm to her days.

Slipped from the palimpsest of her waking hours, that rhythm's absence is now most remarkable.

Celia sits back on the couch, crosses her legs, and rests both hands on her right knee.

She chose to wear the dark blue dress with the

buttons down the back because of the way the colour set off her silver hair. When she was younger, she dressed in pastels, evoking flowers and dawn, her blouses—despite her mother's admonitions—showing just a bit of cleavage.

But at seventy-eight, she selects bold, dark colours that highlight her fair skin and silver hair. Being in mourning is no hardship as far as dress is concerned, and she is glad for the subtle reference to the night sky. It is absurd that so many ladies her age wear flouncy hats and pastels. They dye their hair and go about in ridiculous costume, fooling no one. The triumph of age should be believability. The elderly often do not understand that achieving believability is the only way to avoid being dismissed. Of course, having been endowed with an almost perfect physique, Celia has always enjoyed advantages unavailable to most women, and though her hair is now cropped to a sleek silver helmet, nothing about her appearance obscures her grace. This is an accomplishment. Many older women turn to cruelty to retain a measure of power. Cruelty can hit the mark; it is convincing in a way that love and kindness rarely are. Passion is the hardest to sustain, and it is unbecoming in old age—too grandiose, more like an outburst than the result of a sustainable philosophy.

And love? Well, Celia loved him from girlhood. Even after the night of the terrible game, that love for him beat behind her breastbone like a trapped wasp.

Now he is dead.

"Please shut the window in Senhor Domenico's room, Soccorro. I can hear the chaos from here." Even after five years of living three floors above street level, Celia is still unused to the noise.

Back when they lived in their penthouse overlooking the ocean, only a soft buzz permeated the apartment; it may have been—despite her atheism—the voice of God. Who was to say it was not?

"And I will close the curtain."

"Yes. The curtain in Senhor Domenico's room should remain closed, of course."

From the window in that room, it is possible to see a snippet of the ocean and even a few of the colourful umbrellas along the shoreline. Leaning out, one looks straight down on the awning of the café where—Celia is certain—Domenico met Marisa.

"I am better off when I can see the ocean. I'll stay here," he told her when she asked if he'd like to be moved to the room next to her own so she could check on him more easily. Celia nodded, vaguely remembering some American saying about dust or sand and fingers—a metaphor for waste and loss.

"I never realised how much water there is in the world!" Domenico exclaimed when they first arrived in Brazil after an excruciating boat ride from Italy.

Now the ashes of his body, sucked clean of water, are just a handful. She has no desire to discuss the merits of cremation. In Italy, where the dead are washed, dressed, and laid out in luxurious coffins to be kissed and wept over, few are sympathetic to the practice of burning a body.

Had they a child, that girl or boy would be a grownup now and would be flying in from San Paolo or Brasilia, or maybe even New York City, to come spread the ashes. She would insist that they sit at the dining room table and that the flowers be placed in proximity. She would wear her purple blouse with the sweet neckline evoking in her child a nostalgia for childhood, for being pressed against her bosom, rocked to sleep. They would speak about Domenico, husband, father, imperfect—yes—but "He didn't leave us. We didn't lose the roof over our heads, and we lived comfortably." Celia would have spoken these words out loud, words she had repeated so often to herself. "He didn't leave us." What a relief it would have been to have someone outside herself to comfort. Then she would sit, her hands covering those of her grownup child, speaking of other things but thinking back to the hours they spent together, the humidity of her child's room, the rain outside, the kind circle of lamplight on the books in Italian from a second-hand store, books that had made the same voyage she had made and around the same year, holding her daughter or son against her as they listened to the rain falling with no pattern at all.

But Domenico never wanted children.

Celia glances at the package that Soccorro has brought her; she closes her eyes and takes a sip of coffee.

Soccorro was not quick at learning, but she had eventually succeeded in making a good espresso, rich and dark with a twinge of brutality in the swallow. Before falling ill, Domenico had always assumed the task of brewing coffee, demanding Soccorro's full attention to the process. "When I die," he used to say, "you will have to make it for the Senhora." This remark did not go unappreciated by Celia who, in return, did not compromise on the coffee beans she selected. During their first years together in Rio de Janeiro, Domenico had great difficulty finding Italian espresso beans. Only the most elite boutiques carried them. He would walk to a store on the other side of the city to buy his stock. When Celia pointed out that he hadn't much cared for coffee back in Italy, he said it was not the coffee he needed, but that a lack of coffee recalled the prison camp in Bombay and the Italian prisoners' ritualised exchange of intricate recipes for brewing the best espresso. Celia never pointed out how often in Italy during the war they went without coffee. She preferred that he continued to believe things at home had not been so bad.

"Ah," she sighs, placing her empty cup in its saucer with more clank than necessary. Soccorro does not turn around. Celia stares. Soccorro's bosom is enormous, as though stuffed with a supply of soft fabrics. The rest of

her body is not so large. Her face is a dark cloud
surrounded by the same girlish braids she has always
worn, though now they are streaked in grey.

When Soccorro started working for her, she was
actually slender.

"The coffee was good," Dona Celia says, but to no
avail. She suspects that her servant is hard of hearing
along with her other difficulties. Soccorro is exactly a
year younger than Celia, though she looks much older.
Celia has difficulty recalling life without Soccorro. More
precisely, Soccorro has been with her so long that even
Celia's early life seems infiltrated by Soccorro's presence.
Of course, it is ridiculous to entertain the thought that
Celia is staying in Brazil now because Soccorro is all she
has left. Rio is where she lives. This has become her
home.

Just the other day, a neighbour asked Celia if she
planned on returning to Italy. He had seen the posting in
the elevator about Domenico's death.

Celia was caught off guard. "I live here!"

The man merely nodded.

True, many that emigrated during the war returned to
their hometowns in old age. Returning home, apparently,
was common practice, especially for widows.

But Celia wonders about women who were once as
beautiful as she was. How unbearable to look into the
faces of old acquaintances who ask, "Where have you
been? What was it like living so far away for so long?"
Could she stand, after fifty years of absence, to return to
Montemurro, wrinkled and slow, tolerating the other old
women, once jealous girls, smiling at Time's answer to
age-old prayers?

Though Celia cannot see Soccorro, she knows she is
being watched. She lifts the knife Soccorro placed on the
coffee table and slices through the tape on the box. Both
sides of the box pop open as though having waited too
long for air. "Meo Deus!" Celia exclaims, staring down at

two brown nipples, which stare straight back at her.

Soccorro lumbers over. "My present to you, Senhora."

Celia does not look up. The breasts are lovely and large, twin Cyclops resting at the bottom of a cardboard box, her package.

Soccorro bends down as she has year after year, without urgency or complaint. She manages to pull the bosoms onto her great flank of a forearm then lifts them from the box, holding them as one might a prized fish recently caught and ready for scaling.

Celia feels a vaguely sexual stir at the base of her gut and is surprised at how the room seems to take on a rosy hue. "They're mine," she says in barely a whisper.

Soccorro nods. "They're yours from when I first started working for you." Soccorro lays the breasts gently on the table in front of Celia. "You were vain and haughty then, just like now, not thinking anyone in the world had troubles but you," she goes on in her lilting voice, speaking more words than she does in an average week, "but I didn't think you loved him then. You did love him, and that makes the difference." She brushes one of the plump, firm breasts with the back of her hand. Its nipple hardens visibly.

"They still exist—my breasts from when I was twenty-five or so—right, Soccorro?" Celia asks, looking up now, understanding finally that the unexplored dimensions of her own bosom have always been vaster than she ever imagined, and that she has spent so much of life running her head against the wall of unrequited love that she has never considered a wider range of possibilities for the human heart.

"Go on," Soccorro says, "embrace."

With one stockinged foot, Celia pushes aside the box. She drops to her knees in front of the table, takes in a breath, and nuzzles her face into the soft cleavage of that bosom, her very own. The odour is familiar.

"It may feel strange at first," Soccorro states, watching

over her.

Celia tries to say, no, her bosom here is warm and kind, and there's not one thing to tell it that it doesn't already know. But she falls into a sweet, dreamless sleep.

Sanding the Wood

Therése Halscheid

I know the perfection of white pine
in its natural state of being
unfinished wood,
before the sawing starts
to show the grain, and of areas
disturbing the grain, the circular knots
which surface after
the tree is cut

like what they found
two days ago with some tissue
creeping along, thin membranes
appearing harsh-white
in the x-ray and of that spot
behind the nipple, like a hard knot of wood
that might be removed.

What kind of stain
will I wear, what sheen will it be,
what shape, if the breast is cut back and
cut back, once the skin is pulled taut,
sanded smooth,

this place where your lips fall
on my flesh and stay and stay with
your mouth and move with
your hunger there.

Biopsy

Tammy Nelson

My breasts were trusting this morning
open
soft

They knew that I cared
understood, shot after shot
that we meant them no harm

Now though, the lidocaine wearing off
and the cold pack warm
they give me a wayward glance
ask not to be touched or disturbed

They want an impermeable shield
a layer of protection
and a prayer
that the next touch, be reverential

Soft
as they are

Socialised Medicine

Kathleen McCarty McLaughlin

For weeks, I ignored the ache in my left breast, which told me it was back. I grew tired, barely able to sketch out the next day's English lessons before falling asleep at eight P.M. Intense pain finally made me look at my undressed image in the mirror and admit that my breast was purple and twice the size it should be. I was angry. If it were my toe or even my belly button, it would be all right, but having an infected breast in a foreign country was embarrassing.

I had just begun working at a private language school in Bratislava, and the only people I knew who spoke English fluently were also brand new teachers. My palms sweated as I knocked on the door of Tereska, age fifteen and the best English speaker in our high rise.

As I explained my problem, Tereska's dark brows wrinkled. "Haven't you insurance?"

"No." My legal permit had been delayed by required rounds of Slovak bureaucracy.

"It's a bad time to be sick in Slovakia. We haven't much money."

"I can pay. I just don't know how to explain what's going on."

She dialled her uncle and spoke in Slovak for a while before handing me the phone.

"Katarina. So I hear you have bad breast?" Dr. Hurban bellowed.

"It's infected. I've had this before. I need antibiotics."

"Where you been putting it?" His crackling laugh caused me to pull the phone slightly from my ear.

Tereska made arrangements for me to meet him at the state *nemocnica* (hospital) the next morning.

I stepped from the bus and stared at the sprawling *nemocnica*, the brown-bagged bottle of wine I'd brought as payment clutched against my chest. Early light was rising behind the building, projecting a great shadow into the street, which I crossed slowly, strangely afraid. Following scribbled directions, I found myself in a grey corridor, sharing a bench with three very pregnant women. For two hours, I gazed at a line of pre-op patients on stretchers, inching towards rarely available, creaky elevators.

A dark-haired man stepped into the hallway, and his voice cut through the buzz of words I did not understand. "Who is English?'

Dr. Hurban led me into what looked like a conference room full of nondescript metal chairs then gestured for me to remove my top.

"I've had this before. Twice," I explained as I undid my bra.

"Oh." He shook his head and poked my tender nipple a single time. "Wait. Please!"

Moments later, he returned with another man, also wearing a dark green smock.

They had me step closer to the window, topless, so they could stare at my breast in the light as they smoked cigarettes and debated in Slovak.

At last, Dr. Hurban smiled broadly, conclusively. "Dr. Oravec says we cut!"

It's a bad time to be sick in Slovakia...

I thought of the Canadian teacher who'd had her blood taken at this hospital by a nurse who wasn't wearing gloves.

"I, uh, have to teach in an hour."

"No problem."

I relaxed a little, not realizing then that no problem

meant no anaesthetic.

Dr. Oravec instructed me, through pantomime, to pull green hospital slippers over my shoes and drape a smock around my bare shoulders. Then he slipped a clumsy string of purple beads around my neck and nudged me through a maze of identical grey corridors. I clutched the beads with both hands as pain insisted that I trust these men and fight the urge to run away.

Dr. Oravec pulled on a glove before choosing one of the instruments floating in murky disinfectant while Dr. Hurban placed me on a table and smeared a sallow, acrid solution across my chest.

"Breasts like *Baywatch!*" Dr. Oravec spoke his first and last words of English to me as he pierced my nipple with the scalpel. A fierce and fiery pain shot to my toes. I yelped, but he continued digging until my tongue grew numb as I tried not to scream.

With cotton puffs, Dr. Hurban mopped up the fluids being squeezed from the incision. "Bad. Needs to come out." His bare fingers dangled the soaked cotton inches from my eyeballs. "See? See?" As if proving how necessary the surgery was could calm me down.

To fend off complete panic, I shut my eyes from the sight of my blood, imagining myself asleep.

I couldn't look again until Dr. Oravec was taping a bundle of surgical gauze over the wan, green shunt dangling from my nipple.

Dr. Hurban smiled soothingly and handed me a hand-drawn picture of a breast with a quarter moon etched across its centre. "For your record."

I barely remember dressing or handing him the bottle of wine before floating out of the hospital.

In 1998, Dr. Hurban and Dr. Oravec did something my doctors in the US had not been able to do. The infection was treated so thoroughly that it never returned—and on surgery, medicine, and a necklace, I spent only thirty-three cents.

Missing Parts

Judy Kirk

I had a mole on my right arm
just a few inches above my wrist,
its shape jagged,
the dark brown surface rough and scaly
like tree bark.

It wasn't huge, smaller than a dime
but big enough to catch my eye
when I looked down.

I was certain everyone noticed it
their eyes pulled as eyes can be
to a scar or birthmark.
And the thought of it being cancerous
often crossed my mind.

It was benign.

There's an indentation on my skin
where it had been—no one would
notice but me.

I touch the spot almost daily,
rub it gently and
know a part of me is missing.

I can't begin to fathom
the amount of missing that occurs
when a woman
has her breast removed.

A–Cup

Amy Thompson

You've saved and warmed
your place at the bar,
bottle of Blue Moon chilling
in the cooler. I come—
late like always, you say.
I watch you from the door,
watch every pair of breasts
walk by, as if in slow motion.
Your head orbits planets that
rotate, weave and bounce by—
you look like some bobble-headed
ballplayer in the back window of
a silver Honda Prelude.
Watching you watch them
out of the corner of your blue-grey
eyes, knowing you want them more
than you want me, who lies below you
every night, letting you come
and go when you want—
letting you watch
these breasts, these D-cups,
engrossed and oblivious
to me who now sits right
next you. I feel like nothing
more than tiny peaks
hidden behind Kilimanjaro.

Don't They Come in Pairs?

Michael Bracken

For most teenaged boys, women's breasts are a source of endless fascination.

They were for me, too, but they were much more than that. They were—or, more precisely, their absence was—a primary source of my family's income.

In the late 1960s and through the 1970s, my grandmother managed and later owned a corset shop in Tacoma, Washington, that specialised in fitting mastectomy patients with prosthetic breasts. At various times, my mother and my aunt worked in the shop, and so did I.

The women who visited the shop were of all ages, all social statuses, all races, and all body types. They had been traumatised by mastectomy, radical mastectomy, or double mastectomy, and some wore their scars more obviously than others.

My grandmother, my mother, and my aunt were more than accomplished corsetieres; they were amateur therapists in the best sense. They met the physical needs of women whose cups no longer ranneth over but also met their emotional needs by assuring the women that they could look "normal" again.

What my grandmother could not accomplish with off-the-shelf appliances, she created on one of two Singer sewing machines, altering, adapting, or creating from scratch appliances that matched the women's remaining breasts, and she altered or adapted the brassieres that would hold the appliances to ensure proper fit. When the women walked out of my grandmother's shop, wearing a new prosthetic breast (or pair of breasts), they walked with the confidence that comes from knowing that a casual observer would notice nothing unusual or out of place.

I learned that brassieres and their intended contents weren't something to be snickered about behind the bleachers. More than once, I saw my flat-chested mother or flat-chested aunt don a leotard to model the various brassieres and prosthetic appliances sold in the shop, wearing underwear as outerwear long before Madonna made it fashionable, and I learned to recognise brassieres that were improperly fit, lacked proper support, or had outlived their usefulness at an age when most young men would have been happy just to learn how to unfasten the hooks one-handed.

My role at the shop was to sweep the walk, vacuum the floor, and run errands, tasks I was never particularly good at. If I was present when a customer arrived, I was sent to the back room and instructed to remain there until the customer's needs were met. Sometimes I overheard the women talk, and I learned far more about women's attitudes towards their breasts than I did by listening to the sure-fire methods of reaching second base that my pubescent buddies discussed.

I overheard women who thought they couldn't be real women without their breasts and other women who wouldn't let themselves be defined by their missing body parts. I also overheard stories of women embarrassed to undress in front of their husbands and stories of husbands who refused to even look at their wives post-surgery. More important than that, I learned of marriages strengthened during this time of crisis, of husbands whose support for their wives ensured their successful recovery from mastectomy. I realised that men had just as many different reactions to a spouse's loss of a breast as the women had.

Much has changed since my days working in my

grandmother's corset shop.

Plastic surgeons can rebuild breasts removed by mastectomy, and both prosthetic devices and brassieres have gone hi-tech. What hasn't changed all that much is how we relate to women's breasts.

I'm in my fifties now, and women's breasts still fascinate me, but whether they come in pairs or as singles is immaterial. What matters is the realisation that women are more than the sum of their parts, a lesson I learned by working in my grandmother's corset shop as a teenager.

Radiation Therapy
Ruth Bavetta

Every day
I go to the lowest

level of the hospital,
where I sign in

and sit
with the others.

The television murmurs
in the corner.

The elevator comes
and goes. The fish

swim round
and round

in the aquarium.
One by one

we disappear
behind the heavy

door. One
by one, we come

out, and the fish
swim round

and round
in the bright

artificial
light.

After the War Report

Georgia A. Greeley

It's easier
being a double amputee
like me;
breasts aren't used
to walk or talk
or touch like hands;
their absence
goes
so easily
unnoticed.

Diagnosis

Cary Phillips Auerbach

Each morning, an observant Jew recites a prayer thanking God for once more returning his soul to his body.

There are dreams from which one alights back on earth delicately. The gentlest of these are the seamless kinds that are so interwoven in the texture of wakefulness that they are like droplets dispersed in the day. Or there are dreams from which one crash lands and looks back at a singular conflagration, shocked but relieved. There is yet a third, more ambiguous type.

I am thinking of one such dream of mine—a scene of family tumult, a multifocal frenzy. At the eye of the storm, my bubby sat ensconced in a wing chair. She stilled the ruckus by declaring that she would be going. Then, in a flash of bizarre contortions, she time lapsed through her life in reverse. The last thing I saw was a squirming baby on the seat cushion; I woke just before she vanished into her mother's womb. It was the type of dream from which one staggers awake. It was the type of dream that looks backward and forward.

My own de-evolution began last July with the sinking feeling I had on the day of my annual mammography. Like dreams, presentiments are cracks in the surface of things. And cracks themselves can be premonitions. Probably both are reminders of what we already know on some level but prefer not to think about.

Months earlier, I had said in passing to my husband that I felt like a sitting duck. The comment rolled around on the table for a bit, a foreign coin, worthless for purchase where we lived. The currency suddenly pegged to our own when the radiologist recommended further testing. And a month later, when the biopsy came back positive, the currency in a flash accepted everywhere.

Or perhaps I had uttered this only the week before the mammography, during a much anticipated, years delayed week in Paris, distance standing in for time in my memory.

We interchange time and distance according to our accustomed rate; travel in general, a plane trip in particular, confounds this conversion factor.

My husband, a physician, didn't wait for the biopsy results but called the pathologist himself. He gave me the news when he walked in the door that evening. I was struck by his voice. It was cushioned—like the satin box in which one presents an engagement ring. I nodded. If I had known how to refuse, I would have. My eyes filled just to the brim.

The next day I drove my daughter back to college. I left in the dark—no precise diagnosis, therefore no prognosis, no physician, no treatment plan—and as we drove it grew darker still. By ten o'clock, as we cut across the Adirondacks, it felt as if we were in a bullet hurtling out past our galaxy.

On the other hand, it felt like three hundred miles of back road bushwhacking. Ironically, I attributed its feasibility under emotional duress to the lesser though sufficiently distracting stress of generational discord. The disputations on whether illegal drug use is anti-authoritarian political statement or hedonistic escapism and on the advisability of texting while driving seventy miles per hour agitated me but kept rim-of-the-abyss panic at bay.

I stayed until Saturday to help set up her apartment. It was good to be busy with chores. It was good to be three hundred miles away. It was good to be with my daughter. Yet at the end of the day, the uncertainties of what I faced rose up like bats at dusk. The air felt thick and difficult to breath. I poured sweat when I sat still. I felt completely corporeal and smelly. My daughter had an antiperspirant as strong as embalming fluid to lend me, and I wondered what stressed her out enough to need such a product. I couldn't wait to get home and call a woman I knew who was on the other side of the medical adventure that awaited me.

By early the next week, I had secured an appointment with her surgeon for three weeks hence. Waiting wasn't bad once I had the surgeon, and, not unimportantly, she and her hospital participated in my insurance plan. In the meanwhile: daily life, medical paperwork, phone calls, a continuo of Internet research on treatment options. I called friends, relatives, and relatives of friends who had had a range of diagnoses and a variety of treatments.

One thing about this disease: not only is there cellular proliferation but also proliferation of choice. I've never faced so many consequential decisions in so short a time.

There was, for a non-gambler such as myself, a strange exhilaration in sizing up and playing the odds.

I spoke the most to two women about their experience with breast cancer. P. was the friend whose surgeon I would share. She had a similar history to mine and chose a similar course of treatment. The experience was completely behind her by then, and her pragmatic optimism was a great comfort. L. was a lovely woman who was at this point more a friend of a friend. Her diagnosis coincided with mine, but her history and options were more difficult.

I first called her late one evening, ten days after she had a double mastectomy with no reconstruction. Our mutual friend assured me that it was all right to call so soon. In the course of our conversation, she asked if I had seen the woman online with the elaborate tapestry tattoo in place of her missing breasts.

"No. Google Images hadn't occurred to me."

As we spoke, I began clicking through a gamut of mastectomy and reconstruction images. Although she sympathised with the gasps that escaped me, I'm sure that was not what she wanted to hear ten days after her operation. Over the next few weeks, the pictures offered a new object of contemplation: the ideal breast.

The initial surgical consultation was the day after Labor Day. My husband drove me down to Manhattan but, once there, became so enraged by the traffic that, for the preservation of my equanimity, I slipped out of the car, saying that I should walk so as not to be late.

The surgeon's office was two levels below ground. I descended into a hermetic adobe coloured realm. Beverages and little packages of pretzels, like an anti-septic happy hour, large oil paintings above each seating cluster, high-end magazines fanned out on the tables. In the exam room, a seersucker robe, not standard issue blue paper. A luxury underworld.

The surgeon entered and shook my hand. I studied the scar at the base of her throat. She laid out my options. Importantly, my husband had not yet arrived. At that time, he had been in a jag of talking over me, cutting me off when we spoke with other people as if I required his assistance to be comprehended. I worried that, if he were there initially, a physician short-circuit would have excluded me.

They offered a surgery date on the last Monday in September, but my extended family was to gather at my house then to celebrate the Jewish New Year. I opted for a week delay but, as soon as that date was set, realised that I had jumped from the frying pan into the fire. Yom Kippur began that evening.

Since Yom Kippur is the day God seals the book of life and death until the next New Year, it has a hold on even an unobservant Jew such as me. It's a kind of deadline for atonement.

I fretted over the religious propriety and dithered as to what I should do. In the end, despite lingering doubts, I kept the date.

After the appointment, my husband and I sat by the river and talked things over. I craved another walk—this one, a satisfying two miles down to my parents' apartment. My husband retrieved the car and met me there. Before and after each of my subsequent appointments, I took the opportunity to walk through the city streets. The rhythmic motion, the glorious weather, and the art I sought out on the way beat against my heightened state and linked these interludes into a weird odyssey.

The weather was unremittingly glorious during that September and October. There were no grey, moody days to soften and absorb the experience. Things were thrown into sharp relief, events bounced off the resilient backboard of blue sky and sunshine, at once uplifting and stark. I walked so much and so hard during those months that my feet still ached half a year later.

The prospect of general anaesthesia, its daunting quality of resembling a black hole, propelled me to propose a little jaunt on my "last weekend." I wanted to see my three college aged children before I broached oblivion. My husband and our youngest daughter gamely accompanied me on a seven-hundred-mile trek for a disproportionately brief time with them. Unexpectedly, the distance enhanced the pleasure of the visits. Arduousness and ardour conspired to beatification. The trip's rigors felt like a shriving. The near constant motion engendered a feeling of transport. My husband and my daughter were good sports—or maybe they, too, needed the distraction. We returned Sunday, three days before the operation.

By coincidence, P. had a semi-annual check-up the day before my surgery. I had an appointment that day for sentinel node mapping. She and her close friend drove me down to New York. I curled up in the back seat; its black leather and canted privacy windows created a cocoon. The congenial conversation up front carried me along like a river of chant. In the city, we shared a light lunch of soup and California rolls and discussed the vagaries of suburban parenting. I wasn't hungry and went along only to be sociable. I rarely took lunch out, and it all had the sense of a lark. I saved my fortune cookie for later.

After lunch, I hugged the women farewell—we were that close by then—and walked uptown to my appointment. Overhead in a crowded, slightly dingy waiting room, Bernanke talked about fiscal implosion, as I saw to loose ends regarding insurance and pre-operative test results, heedless of the cell phone minutes expended. At last they summoned me. A brief history, directions to lie on my back, gown open to the front. The radioactive substance injected into my axilla stung. I was dismissed and instructed to return in two hours.

As it happened, L. was also in town. She had suggested that we meet while she waited for her chemotherapy session. She participated in an experimental protocol of an intensive, shorter treatment. The close monitoring meant more waiting time, more time for a visit.

The office was one floor above my surgeon's, still in that buried place. As I wandered the windowless maze looking for her, a small white face behind round black glasses and beneath two hats riveted me. The elfin figure had a fey look and spoke with a piping, disembodied voice to a perky social worker.

At that moment, my cell phone rang; because I was underground, all I could do was listen. My responses were not heard. My friend continued anyway, in an act of faith, to pour forth words of love and support. My head and heart were there in the river of his words, while my eyes continued to stray over the alien precinct.

More circling. I hadn't seen L. in many years, and I realised I might not recognise her. I entered the therapeutic arena and checked the cubicles arrayed radially along the perimeter. This sliding glimpse of geometrised illness, the proliferation of patients and medical personnel was vertiginous. It felt as if I had dipped for a moment beneath the normal plane, as if the skin of the moment were peeled back to reveal what pulsed beneath but was never seen.

I asked for her at various reception desks and searched still as I heard her warm, Hebraic voice call my name. There, immediately familiar, the open smiling face, the lambent green eyes, faded freckle complexion akin to my own family's—probably remotely connected, centuries back in the old country, some genetic fragments in common. There, her husband, his image revised in the moment with whiter hair. L. and I settled together on one couch, while he retreated with his laptop. We immediately fell into intimate conversation.

L.'s situation differed from my own in that my strong family history suggested a genetic cause, whereas her breast cancer was most likely fallout from radiation treatment for Hodgkin's disease. At age sixteen, she had discovered a lump in her neck while dressing. As she recounted that lost year, she remarked that her daughters, at fifteen and eighteen, straddled that time for her. Similarly, my youngest, just on the point of adolescence, by symmetry helped bracket a passing phase of my life.

Earlier radiation precluded L. from getting implants, the course I had partly chosen. She did not want the complicated surgery and long recovery of the autologous option. She was adamant in the face of her husband's doubt. Yet despite his ultimate support and what our mutual friend described as her utter lack of vanity, L. had a bad reaction when she first returned home. Her ravaged chest horrified her. It wasn't too long after that my gasps had assaulted her through the telephone.

"Well," I observed, "there is one upside to mastectomy. You can claim to have had beautiful, round breasts, like the fish that got away."

Our talk digressed to this and that and at last to her worry about her eldest's diffidence, L.'s fear that she would fail to capitalise on her artistic talent. Her daughter loved all that was fine and pure and unapplied.

"Ah," I responded. "A child after my own heart."

If there is even a remote possibility that some activity of mine might result in financial reward, I seem to run screaming from the room. Some little avatar of fear tucked in my primitive being is the culprit, no doubt.

I noticed that the double-hatted woman had moved and now sat opposite us. She repeatedly stuffed a small white dog back into a zippered carrying case. We smiled at the squirming contraband.

"She's usually not so jumpy," she said with an impish look.

She seemed more earthbound now. The conversation turned to diagnoses and treatments. She felt herself to be extremely lucky that this institution pioneered the protocol for her aggressive HER2[4] tumour.

"It's interesting how we redefine luck," I observed.

As I sat among all the chemotherapy patients, I kept thinking the nurses called my name. At this point I didn't know if I would need chemo. I wondered if it was bad juju to sit there.

When it was time for me to go back uptown for my lymph node mapping, I bid L. and her husband goodbye. After another dingy wait, a young technician led me to a room and onto a narrow platform where I was told to lie on my back and raise my arms above my head. I was rolled into a machine that photographed me. The beauty of the resulting image stunned me. My black silhouette, waist up, arms upraised, showed a fantastically bright

---

[4] Human Epidermal growth factor Receptor 2

star on my chest, two smaller glows near my armpit. It looked like Matisse. I wanted to frame it and call it "Etoile." I would have no compunction selling it for lots of money because truly I felt it would give someone his money's worth. The image looked like aspiration, like transfiguration, like flight and transcendence.

I walked the two and half miles down to my parents' apartment. I figured it would be my last good walk for a while. They indulged me with a meal at their neighbourhood Italian restaurant: fresh bread, red wine, red snapper with spinach, salad, garlic spaghetti, and cappuccino. Fasting after midnight was a cinch.

I rose at five A.M. from a dreamless sleep (the operation was scheduled for 7:30). I moved through that dim hour, deprived of my habitual coffee. When my mother and I went down to the street to catch a cab to the hospital, I wore no makeup, carried no personal effects, and, although I had recited no prayer, I was deeply cognisant of my bare soul in my naked body.

In the Breast

Julene Tripp Weaver

—for Negesti

I.
where the heart
blessed sleeps
resting calm
fast growth
myeloma
      what is the
      distinction
breast plate to
      vein
      to artery
      pumping
canyons run
strong blood gushes
across boulders
under caverns
and the fire tornados
from your fifth chakra

baby child
next to water
pen in hand
you sculpt this world
on a blank page
falling yourself, eager
to explore
you must
      you must

II
The cancer caught you
The cancer, fast growth
multiplying cells

Our wars inside
replicate like those outside
we have no choice

a slime mould steady-growth
                    death weave

a chance you took
to cherish each minute,
words you sang to us

to think I loved
all of you—including
the cancer deep in your breast

rabid as a dog gone
mad, you railed your
poems into the world
publishing pushing

all our love filling you
filling your cancer, too

III.
It is a born razor
what took you out
A born lose tie
looped into noose

The red chair you sat in
too soon and never rose
the catatonic spell
you went under

A long mowed down
explanation

as if school could have
taught you how to cope
with this cancer war

I love how you rose
up singing songs out of
ancient hymnals—
how dastardly
you rode the
shackles of bodily
limitations—the liberation
you found in death—
razor sharp
your words
sting

Growing Breasts for Spider-Man
Rachel Furey

Riley has her hands clamped over her pale, bare breasts when her father barges into the bathroom without knocking. He grabs a tube of Neosporin then quickly exits the room. Riley is not mad; she cannot afford to be mad. Her friend Sandra has informed her that anger can be debilitating toward growth. There in the bathroom, her breasts barely filling her small cupped hands, she knows that getting angry is not a chance she can take right now. She has seen the chests of the girls in her class, and none of them are as meagre as hers. In fact, she swears they are growing by the day, blossoming into prominent round beings that bounce under their sweaters and catch the eyes of boys as they tread through the hallways. She is sure it is these round beings that make the girls smile so widely and give them the nerve to occasionally talk back to their teachers.

When Riley collapses onto her bed at night, she thinks, perhaps if her chest were larger, all her problems would slip away, because Sandra has assured her this is a possibility. Sandra has told her that womanhood is a precious thing, and it's only a matter of time before Riley steps into it. When she closes her eyes, Riley tries to imagine rounded hills, filled water balloons heavy with the weight of liquid, kick balls ripe with air, puffer fish all blown up, bocce balls, and expanded air bags—anything round and large, anything she might dream of, anything that could inspire her chest to begin to grow.

At the breakfast table, her father flashes a foolish smile. "It's never too early," he says, "for your first self

137

breast exam."

If his hands were not so anxious as he pours her glass of orange juice, if his eyes didn't shine with the pride of a man who thinks his daughter has already begun checking herself for signs of cancer, Riley would reach out a hand and smack him across his narrow face because she is only twelve years old and twelve-year-olds have a long list of things to worry about (boys, breasts, pimples, schoolwork, breasts, periods, boys, and breasts), but cancer is not anywhere even remotely close to that list, and Riley does not need such a word burdening her already burdened mind.

She drinks the orange juice her father hands her, hoping that, through its pulp and its vitamins, it might encourage a little more growth in that area where her blouses are baggy and loose.

At school, Riley finds Sandra huddled in the back of a bathroom stall, pushing tissues into her bra. This obsession with breasts, with boobs, bosoms, and busts, is not something that has hit Riley alone; it is a wildfire that has spread through the grade, igniting boys and girls alike.

"How big do you think Patrick likes 'em?" Sandra asks.

Riley can only shove her hands into her pockets and bite her tongue. How is she to know what size the quarterback of the seventh grade football team best likes his breasts when she cannot even urge her own to grow? She watches Sandra's left hand dive into her T-shirt and bra. Small, round globes begin to emerge beneath Sandra's Abercrombie T-shirt. Riley eyes her own breasts, wondering if they, too, could benefit from this padding. But she doesn't currently have her eye on a guy, or at least not one who walks these school hallways, one she could add an extra layer of tissues for each day until he notices, the way Sandra is doing. Riley's guy goes beyond just the school walls and beyond state lines or even national boundaries.

She has a crush on Spider-Man—not the cartoon character, but the one in the movie, the one played by Tobey Maguire. She hasn't even told Sandra about this crush yet because it's troublesome to explain.

Riley is not in love with simply the character, or simply Tobey Maguire, because he just isn't the same in *Seabiscuit*, a movie that drones helplessly on while, during each race scene, Riley waits for Tobey to spit webbing from his wrists and quickly hop from horse to horse until he finds himself in the very front of the pack, dashing across the finish line first and earning a bouquet of flowers he could hand over to her.

No, Riley is in love with the Spider-Man/Tobey Maguire combination.

And when, from inside the bathroom stall, Sandra again asks Riley if she might want to try stuffing her bra today, Riley turns her down because she's thinking of the day a stranger approaches her on her walk home from school and, with a fake smile and thick arms, tries to muscle her into his car. Or the day their chemistry teacher, Mrs. Susanna, finally loses it and sets all the Bunsen burners aflame at once, the chemistry classroom going up in conflagration, and Spider-Man, in his sleek red and blue suit, is there to rescue to her, to scoop her up in his strong arms and whip her off to safety. Then, as they fly together, suspended by his sturdy strands of webbing, she will hug him tight, feeling his muscles under his suit, and whisper into his ear, "Forget Kirsten Dunst. Look at this chest. Look at how light and aerodynamic it is, how easily we can fly together." Riley, like Sandra, has her story, too.

But Riley's is not so easy to believe in the locker room before gym class, when she must change with all the other girls, the girls who sport B or C or even size D bras—or at the very least can fill an A.

Sometimes she wishes for Spider-Man to come then, to string up some of these girls and let them hang from the ceiling a moment, mummified in webbing and shrieking in fright, a moment that would maybe remind them that they, too, are human. She would never ask too much of Spider-Man, just that he keep these girls in line, that he maybe cause a mysterious explosion or two in Mrs. Susanna's classroom, and that every now and then he could steal her father away when he yet again eavesdrops on a phone conversation or lingers at her back when she's checking her email. She knows it would only take suspending him from the office building across town or even the flag pole at the school, just once, to teach him better.

But Spider-Man has not arrived yet, so she must continue on without him, and that means quickly changing her T-shirt while some of the other girls, bare stomached, their breasts round under grown-up bras (the kind with the hook in the back that Riley still isn't sure she can work) linger in the process. They act as if they can't find their gym shirts inside their lockers and stand tall and let out sighs that make their chests rise and fall with the sound until, at last, they pull out their shirts and slip them on and, even then, stand for a moment with their hands on their hips, staring at the form of their chests under the fabric in admiration, their eyes twinkling and their mouths curving into shy smiles. It is these moments that, at barely five feet tall and one hundred pounds, Riley feels the smallest. She has to bend her chin all the way to her sternum to see her chest and cannot stare down at any part of herself in admiration and awe. She can only stare down at her body in frustration, trying to will it to grow.

They are in the middle of their volleyball unit in gym class, and this does not help matters any because Riley can't even serve the damn ball over the net. Every time, the ball falls hopelessly short, plummeting to the ground yards before crossing the net. Their physical education teacher, Mrs. Morely, has a large, supple chest that shows under anything she wears, and she can serve the ball well over the net, landing it in the very back corner of the court. Because of this, Riley believes muscle and power and serving and breasts are all interconnected in ways she may not ever completely comprehend, but she understands enough to know that her chest must—must must must—grow.

Sandra and Riley have worked out the system of not standing in line next to each other because Mrs. Morely always counts off in twos to make teams; by letting one person jump in line between them, they end up on the same team, both of them helplessly treading the warm-up lap behind the others on their team. Sandra does not shed her fake chest even for gym class, and Riley can hear the shifting of the tissues as she runs. She can see them taking on a new shape beneath Sandra's T-shirt. Riley should say something because she knows no good can come from this. But Sandra is smiling, the flimsy, light breasts somehow managing to please her and to create the confidence that beams in the faces of the bustier girls. So Riley bites her tongue and jogs and tries not to run out of breath.

While Riley sits and waits her turn to enter the game, she searches the high gymnasium ceiling for Spider-Man's lurking red and blue form, looking for him nestled somewhere in the rafters. She hopes he is practicing the aim of his webbing so that, following Riley's serve, he can tug the ball over the net, perhaps in the process slapping someone like Christine or Britney in the face with it so they tumble backward and that, for once, they'll be who the class laughs at.

When she does not find him, Riley thinks of him during her serve anyway, as if the mere thought of him might enhance her serve, giving her the power she needs to lift the ball over the net. Riley leaves her left hand outstretched, the ball balanced there, then whips back her right to kick it forward and lift the ball into the air, where it slowly sails toward the net, floating as if it's a beach ball with nowhere to go. And again, despite Riley's willings, despite her praying at night, asking God if maybe just once he could lift the ball over the net for her, it falls short, thudding to the gymnasium floor a few feet before the net. Two of the girls turn to glare at Riley, but most of them are accustomed to her short serves, so she does not have to shoulder too many terrible looks while she waits for the serve from the other side of the court.

It is Britney's turn to serve, and, because her chest is large and her eyes confident and her arm strong, she serves the ball overhand and still manages to get it over the net. The ball plummets toward Sandra's knees. With tight lips and a concentrated gaze, Sandra dips her knees the way Mrs. Morley has instructed them to do, the way Riley and Sandra usually try to avoid but now, in this moment that just might grant them the opportunity for revenge, must. Sandra squeezes her forearms together and extends them, the ball seeming to aim right for them. She takes another step forward, and the ball ricochets against her chest, a spray of tissues rising from the collar of her T-shirt. The pieces slowly flutter to the ground as if they are homemade snow.

Even yards behind her, Riley can feel Sandra's blood boil as giggles begin to spurt from the girls. Britney raises a finger in the air to mark her scored point while twirling a curl of her blonde hair.

It's the kind of moment that makes Riley wish she had a booming voice that could carry across a gymnasium and make people stop and listen. Perhaps then she would grasp her chest the way her father caught her doing this morning in the mirror and dare to ask, "What is wrong with these?"

But Riley's mouth is dry and her stomach anxious, and she searches the rafters once more for Spider-Man and his lean, vibrant form, the reflection of his eyes, before shuffling to Sandra's side, where she scoops up the tissues still warm from the heat of her friend's body. Sandra is frozen in place like a statue, her arms still outstretched the way they were when the ball hit. Her eyes are wet and the corners of her mouth drooping down as Riley plucks a half-seen tissue from the collar of her T-shirt and pushes her arms back down. She curls her hand into one of Sandra's and tugs her friend toward the locker room, even as Mrs. Morley calls them back and cites the dip in their grades this early exit will cause.

In the bathroom stall, Sandra cries. Riley can hear her gentle, croaking sobs and does not remind Sandra that this is where it all started. She leans in against the cool metal door and considers suggesting that maybe Patrick likes a flat chest, but she is not so naïve to think this is true.

"You're lucky," Sandra says. "Lucky you're not in love."

But Riley is. She's in deep, head-over-heels kind of love with the Spider-Man/Tobey Maguire combination and all the possibilities that come with it.

Riley wants to tell Sandra she is the lucky one because she's chosen someone inside the school walls, someone she sees not only in her dreams or on television but in an actual classroom. She wants to tell Sandra that she has a better chance of reeling in her love than Riley does.

But instead, because the other girls will be coming back into the locker room soon, because Sandra needs to know she is not the only one with a farfetched love, Riley tells her about Spider-Man. She says she's been dreaming of him ever since she saw the first movie. She says she's still waiting for him to appear at her windowsill and whip her off into the night, perhaps flying her to Dairy Queen for a Blizzard, because this is her favourite fantasy—Spider-Man keeping her warm with his muscled arms while she dips her spoon into a Chocolate Xtreme Blizzard and feels the sugar sizzle into her bloodstream.

The bathroom door creaks open. On the other side, Sandra is smiling, the corners of her mouth tickling upward then letting go in a laugh that sails its way into the locker room, echoing off the concrete floors and metal lockers. She laughs so hard she tips forward and places a hand on her stomach. "Thanks," she says, patting Riley on the back as if it were all a joke, as if she had not divulged one of her favoured secrets but instead made up a tale for her friend.

Riley swallows and manages a weak smile, for once not pulled into the contagion of Sandra's laugh.

When the other girls file back into the locker room, Riley and Sandra pull their clothes from their lockers and begin to change.

"Spider-Man," Sandra is still whispering incredulously under her breath.

The other girls eye them, and Riley and Sandra stay quiet, neither willing to spill the other's story of love. There in the chilly locker room, each of the other girls so focused on herself that Riley knows they will never see, she pulls off her small bra and pulls her T-shirt back into place. She wonders if maybe this will give them space to grow, if maybe now they will move a little more under her shirt and the boys will notice.

Pulling her hair into a ponytail, Sandra eyes Riley's chest. Then she whispers into Riley's ear, "They do look a little bigger now."

And yet still, secretly, Riley waits for Spider-Man, waits for him to scoop her into his arms and lift her from the face of this world and into a new one.

What's Your Story?

_____

_____

_____

_____

_____

_____

_____

_____

_____

_____

_____

_____

_____

_____

_____

_____

_____

_____

_____

_____

_____

_____

_____

Contributor Bios

Betty Dobson is the owner/operator of InkSpotter Publishing, as well as a published and award winning writer. She is also a long-time member of Zonta International, an organization dedicated to improving the status of women.

Darcelle Adams-Frank is a student support worker with a long history in social services and a promising future as a teacher. She is one of the driving forces behind this anthology, which marks her first foray into the world of publishing.

Cary Phillips Auerbach is a writer and visual artist in the Hudson Valley, New York. She began writing while home raising her children. She writes poetry and essays and has a first draft novel patiently awaiting revision.

Shawn Aveningo was voted one of The Best Poets in the 2009 Sacramento News & Review Reader Poll. Her poetry has appeared in numerous publications, and she has been a featured performer at various venues throughout California. Shawn has four published books—*She Has Something to Say, Stripped, And Life Goes On...,* and *Because Red is Your Favorite Color*—which are available at ThePoetryBox.com. Shawn's a Show-Me girl from Missouri, graduated Summa Cum Laude from University of Maryland, and is a very proud mother of three.

Ruth Bavetta is a poet and artist whose work has been

shown nationwide. Her poems have appeared in *Nimrod, Poetry East, Tar River Review, Rattle, North American Review, Spillway, Hanging Loose, Rhino*, and *Poetry New Zealand*, among others, and is included in the anthology *Twelve Los Angeles Poets*.

Lois Jean Bousquet's essays appear in *Press Pause Moments: Essays about Life Transitions by Women Writers* (Anne Witkavitch) and *In Their Own Voices* (Oregon Writers Colony). She also teaches writing to seniors. A full-length book on elder independence is in progress. Lois Jean lives in Albany, Oregon, with husband, Dennis, her best friend.

Even though he is the author of several books—including the young adult romance *Just in Time for Love* and the hardboiled private eye novel *All White Girls*—**Michael Bracken** is better known as the author of almost 900 short stories. CrimeFictionWriter.blogspot.com and CrimeFictionWriter.com

An MFA in poetry student at Oxford's fabulous Ole Miss, **Wendy Buffington** has been a waitress, attorney, copy editor, tea shop owner, and cross-country cyclist, riding from Florida to Alaska via Mexico. Her chapbook, *Untied*, was a finalist for the Peter Meinke Poetry Prize. She lives in Florida and Maine.

Rick Bursky's most recent book, *Death Obscura*, is out from Sarabande Books. His previous book, *The Soup of Something Missing*, was published by Bear Star Press. His poems have appeared in many journals. Bursky teaches poetry at UCLA Extension. You can read his blog at rickbursky.blogspot.com.

Sharon Burton is based in Southern California. When she's not writing creative non-fiction, she's consulting with clients, teaching technical communication at the local University of California, or speaking publicly. Sharon also knits, gardens, and hangs out with her writer husband. www.sharonburton.com

Sarah Werthan Buttenwieser's work has recently appeared in *Brain Child Magazine, Huffington Post, The New Haven Review,* and various anthologies, including *The Maternal is Political* (Seal Press). She keeps a blog called *Standing in the Shadows* and writes for *Preview Massachusetts Magazine* regularly. She's a graduate of Hampshire College and the MFA Program for Writers at Warren Wilson College.

Ann Cefola is the author of *St. Agnes, Pink-Slipped* (Kattywompus Press, 2011), *Sugaring* (Dancing Girl Press, 2007), and the translation *Hence this cradle* (Seismicity Editions, 2007). She is a recipient of the Witter Bynner Translation Residency Award at the Santa Fe Art Institute, as well as the Robert Penn Warren Award judged by Pulitzer Prize-winning poet John Ashbery. www.anncefola.com.

Sarah Conover has authored five books on world wisdom traditions and the spiritual education of families. She has an MFA in poetry from Eastern Washington University and has published poems in numerous literary magazines and anthologies. At fifty-five, she is still fascinated by how men and women perform their gender.

J.M. Cornwell fell in love with words long before falling in love with Victoria's Secret. Her first novel, *Past Imperfect*, debuted in July 2009, and her second, *Among Women*, in April 2011. She lives in the shadow of Pikes Peak, writing stories for anthologies and book reviews for Authorlink.

Barbara Daniels' *Rose Fever* was published by WordTech Press. She received two Individual Artist Fellowships from the New Jersey Council on the Arts and earned an MFA in poetry at Vermont College.

Carol Dorf's poems have appeared in *Sin Fronteras*, *Spillway*, *Hip Mama: The Parenting Zine*, *The Mom Egg*, *In Posse Review*, *Moira*, *The Prose Poem Project*, *Feminist Studies*, *Heresies*, *Fringe*, *The Midway*, *Poemeleon*, *Runes*, and *13th Moon*. They have been anthologized in *Not a Muse*, *Boomer Girls*, and elsewhere.

Janice A. Farringer lives in Chapel Hill, North Carolina, where she is at work on her new novel. Her piece "Biopsy" also appears in the anthology *Voices of Breast Cancer*, LaChance Publishing, October 2007.

Rachel Furey is a PhD student at Texas Tech. She is a winner of *Sycamore Review*'s Wabash Prize for Fiction and *Crab Orchard Review*'s Charles Johnson Student Fiction Award. Her work has also appeared in *Women's Basketball Magazine*, *Freight Stories*, *Waccamaw*, *Terrain*, *Hunger Mountain*, *The Prose Poem Project*, and *Sweet*.

Georgia A. Greeley is a writer and visual artist, interdisciplinary in thought and creative action. Making her own books offers her a vessel that can hold an almost unlimited variety of media, text, and images, allowing so much more than one single work of art. And yet it is one single work of art. A lovely paradox. She is hooked on books, whether she writes them or makes them from scratch. georgiaagreeley-artichokepress.com

Thérése Halscheid is the author of three poetry collections, *Powertalk*, *Without Home*, and *Uncommon Geography*, which was a finalist for the 2007 Paterson Poetry Book Prize. She received a Greatest Hits Award from Pudding House and a 2003 Fellowship for Poetry from New Jersey State Council on the Arts. Her poems and stories have appeared in numerous journals. She is a visiting writer in schools and teaches at Atlantic Cape Community College, New Jersey.

Rose Hammond is the pseudonym of a writer who prefers to remain anonymous.

Emily Hayes received her MA in English Literature from Southern Illinois University, Carbondale. Currently, she teaches English at Carbondale Community High School and Morthland College in West Frankfort, Illinois. She is the co-editor for *The Village Pariah*, and her works have previously appeared or are forthcoming in various journals, including *Review Americana, Paterson Literary Review, Diverse Voices Quarterly, Ruminate, Naugatuck River Review*, and *Broad River Review*.

Jenni L. Ivins' career spans the Arts in myriad genres from writing to visual arts. Her work has won prizes and placements. It has been published globally in books, magazines and newspapers, in public art exhibitions, on the radio and internet. Jenni performs on stage in spoken word, choir, and amateur theatre.

Roberta Beach Jacobson is an American author and humorist who makes her home on the remote Greek island of Karpathos. She coauthored the award-winning *Almost Perfect: Disabled Pets and the People Who Love Them* (Enspirio House, an imprint of Word Forge Books). RobertaBeachJacobson.com

Judy Kirk retired from an advertising career and now writes poetry and teaches memoir writing classes at libraries throughout Minnesota. She has published two chapbooks, and her poetry has appeared in *Whispering*

Angel anthologies and *Talking Stick*, a Minnesota literary magazine. She is a graduate of Indiana University and lives in St. Louis Park, Minnesota.

Daisy Levy is a doctoral candidate in Embodied Rhetorics from Michigan State University and has a MA in Creative Writing from Miami University. Her work has appeared in *Limestone: Journal of Art and Literature*, *Plantarchy*, *smallspiralnotebook*, and *Fourth Genre: Explorations in Non Fiction*.

Mary MacGowan was born in Michigan, moved out east where she raised three children, now she's back in her home state, singing about love and lakes. She studied music and composition at Interlochen Arts Academy and NYU. She's a widely published poet, with poems in over forty literary journals, including *The South Carolina Review*, *The Literary Review*, *POEM*, *Cimarron Review*, *The Orange Willow Review*, *Westview*, *Blood Orange*, *Apple Valley Review*, and *Review Americana*. She has a master's degree in Art Therapy and Creativity Development and really does sit by the lake every day to watch the ducks swim by.

Kathleen McCarty McLaughlin's writing has appeared in *Denver Quarterly*, *Tea Party Magazine*, and Web del Sol's *In Posse* Review. Her manuscript *BURN* received a special mention in the 2009 FC2 Ronald Sukenick/ *American Book Review* Innovative Fiction Con-test. She currently resides in Phoenix, Arizona.

Maria Nazos is the author of *A Hymn That Meanders* (Wising Up Press). Her work is published or forthcoming in *The Raleigh Review*, *The Boxcar Poetry Review*, *The Chicago Quarterly Review*, *Poet Lore*, *The New York Quarterly*, *The Sycamore Review*, and elsewhere. She lives in Provincetown, Massachusetts.

For **Tammy Nelson**, writing is a spiritual practice. She began with journal entries, progressed to poetry, and now is learning the guitar and creating songs. In the Winter of 2010, Tammy began a daily practice of writing five gratitudes, some of which she shares at becometheprayer.blogspot.com.

Native Detroiter **Christina Pacosz**'s poetry/writing has appeared in books, literary magazines, and online journals for half a century. *Notes from the Red Zone*, originally published by Seal Press (1983), was the inaugural winner of the ReBound Series (Seven Kitchens Press, 2009). *How to Measure the Darkness* will launch the Seven Kitchens Summer 2012 Limited Edition Chapbook Series.

Andrea Potos is the author of three poetry collections, including *Yaya's Cloth* (Iris Press) and *Abundance to Share with the Birds* (Finishing Line Press). Another full-length collection, *We Lit the Lamps Ourselves*, is forthcoming in 2012 from Salmon Poetry in Ireland.

Kerry-lyn Radloff, South African born, currently lives and works in Tanzania, East Africa. Writing—poetry and prose—is a means to calm a savage and restless soul—especially as her husband is on the high seas more often than not and her daughters have left Africa to attend universities overseas. In addition to writing, Kerry-lyn paints and works as an interior designer for safari lodges in East Africa. In the absence of man and children, Kerry-lyn's companions are Meme-the-Mad, Kuku, Harriet, Mouse-the-mostly-brave, and Biltong Jones. These animals—three dogs and two cats—appear in her illustrated children's books.

Robert R. Sanders is a brilliant photographic visionary who has mentored thousands of photographers during his more than thirty-year professional career in commercial, fine art, and portraiture photography. As an artist who believes in giving back to the community, he's thrilled to contribute his artistic interpretation to the cause.

Linda Simone's poems and essays have appeared in print and online journals and anthologies. Her fifteen-poem sequence, "Stations of the Cross," was nominated for a Pushcart Prize. Her chapbook, *Cow Tippers*, won the Shadow Poetry Chapbook competition. She has also published poems and a picture book, *Moon*, for children.

Amy Thompson taught English and writing before becoming a freelance writer. Her poetry, fiction, and non-fiction, have been published in many journals and magazines. She currently resides in South Dakota with her family and owns Prairie Fire Gallery and Studio, her own art gallery. She is currently working on her second book of poems, *Giving Up My Ghosts: The Women I Carry*.

Julene Tripp Weaver, a former New Yorker, has a private counselling practice in Seattle. Her book, *No Father Can Save Her,* was published by Plain View Press this year. She is widely published in journals, and her chapbook, *An AIDS Case Manager Wails Her Blues*, is based on her work through the heart of the AIDS epidemic. She does wordplay on Twitter @trippweavepoet and has a website at julenetrippweaver.com.

Christine Valentine lives in Montana, writes poetry and non-fiction, and is published in many anthologies. She is editor for the *WyoPoets' Newsletter*. Chris was imported from England in 1964 and has not yet reached her sell-by date.

Davi Walders' poetry and prose have appeared in more

than 200 anthologies and journals. Her collection *Women Against Tyranny: Poems of Resistance During the Holocaust* was published by Clemson University Digital Press in 2011. She developed the Vital Signs Writing Project at NIH in Bethesda, MD, for which she received Hadassah of Greater Washington's Myrtle Wreath Award. Other awards include a National Endowment for the Humanities Grant, a Puffin Foundation Grant, a Maryland State Artist Grant in Poetry, a Luce Foundation Grant, and fellowships to Ragdale Foundation, Blue Mountain Center, and Virginia Center for the Creative Arts. Her work has been read by Garrison Keillor on Writer's Almanac and nominated for Pushcart Prizes.

Patricia Wellingham-Jones is a former psychology researcher and writer/editor with an interest in healing writing and the benefits of writing and reading work together. Widely published, she writes for the review department of *Recovering the Self: a journal of hope and healing* and has ten chapbooks of poetry.

Martha Witt is the author of the critcally acclaimed novel *Broken As Things Are* (Holt; 2004/Picador; 2005). Her translations and short fiction are included in the anthologies *Post-War Italian Women Writers* (Northwestern University Press), *The Literature of Tomorrow* (Rinehart, Holt, and Winston), and *This Is Not Chick Lit* (Random House), as well as *One Story Magazine*, *The Chattahoochee Review*, *Boulevard Magazine*, *Harpur Palate*, and many other national literary journals. As a Thomas J. Watson Traveling Fellow, she spent a year interviewing and writing about Italian women writers. Her interviews and articles have been published in *Leggere Donna*. She is also the recipient of a Spencer Fellowship, a Walter E. Dakin Fellowship, a New York Times Writing Fellowship, a McCracken Fellowship, and The John Gardner Award for Short Fiction, as well as residencies at the Yaddo, Ragdale, Elea Wassard, and Virginia Center for the Creative Arts artist colonies. She is currently an Assistant Professor of Creative Writing at William Paterson University in Wayne, New Jersey.

Mary Zelinka lives in the Willamette Valley and works at the Center Against Rape and Domestic Violence in Corvallis, Oregon. Her writing has appeared in *CALYX*, *Open Spaces*, *Pilgrimage*, and *The Sun*.

www.ingramcontent.com/pod-product-compliance
Lightning Source LLC
Chambersburg PA
CBHW021108090426
42738CB00006B/550